Montessori Made Easy:
Practical Life Lessons

A Guide for Parents, Teachers, Preschools, and Child Care Centers for Creating Activities and Teaching Practical Life Skills using Simple Inexpensive Materials

Andrea Hendon Busch, Ed.D.

Dedication

This book is dedicated to all young children; wishing each of them a childhood filled with the joys and benefits of Montessori Practical Life experiences.

Montessori Made Easy:
Practical Life Lessons

A Guide for Parents, Teachers, Preschools, and Child Care Centers for Creating Activities and Teaching Practical Life Skills using Simple Inexpensive Materials

Copyright © 2013 Andrea Hendon Busch, Ed.D.

All rights reserved.

No part of this book may be generated or transmitted in any form or by any means, electronic or mechanical, including photocopying, recording, or by any information storage or retrieval system, without the permission of the publisher.

Published by
Building Blocks Books
P.O. Box 623, Liverpool, TX 77577

Acknowledgements

I am grateful to Janella Hendon and Scott Phillips for their editing of this book. I greatly appreciate the hours they each spent reading and providing input into the quality of this book. I also appreciate the opportunity to work with many children and families over the years. I've enjoyed the opportunities to develop curriculum and activities for children and watch them enjoy the processes of learning.

Notice to the Reader

This book is designed to provide ideas of how to develop and teach Montessori Practical Life skills. The information provided should be used within the readers own context, good judgment, and appropriate usage of materials. Materials should always be appropriate based on the age and developmental level of the child. In addition, the choice to use materials must be carefully evaluated within the framework of whether the activities are completed at home with a parent or in a licensed child care center. Parents have more liberal options than teachers and child care workers those operating within a school or licensed child care center. In these cases teachers must be careful to observe all relevant choices of lessons and materials within the scope of their licensing regulations.

Despite the best efforts of both the author and publisher, the book may contain mistakes, either typographical or in content. The reader is solely responsible for actions taken within his or her own early childhood program. This relates to all subject matter including both theory and practice. This book is sold without warranties of any kind and the publisher and author are not responsible for any liability, loss, or damages from the reader's use of the book and its content.

CONTENTS

Introduction 1

Chapter 1: What is Practical Life 5

Chapter 2: Environment and Presentation 9

Chapter 3: Scooping and Transferring 15

Chapter 4: Pouring and Transferring 29

Chapter 5: Sifting and Straining 41

Chapter 6: Food Preparation 44

Chapter 7: Cleaning and Organizing 66

Chapter 8: Care of Self and Others 75

Chapter 9: Art and Design 83

Chapter 10: Construction 98

Chapter 11: Nature and Outdoors 103

Appendix A: Grace and Courtesy 110

Appendix A: Safety Lessons 110

Appendix B: Material Sources for Building Your Practical Life Program 111

Introduction

Introduction

Montessori Practical Life activities are some of the most basic and yet some of the most beneficial and enjoyable activities for building skills in young children. Although Montessori programs often include expensive materials and set up requirements, there are many activities which can be created using simple, inexpensive, and easily accessible materials. Practical Life easily fits into these criteria. All of the ideas presented in the book were put together for less than $10.00 each. Many of the activities can be put together at little or no cost by utilizing items that you already have around your house or in your child care center. If the exact materials aren't readily available, simply find something else that works. Look around for everyday materials that you can either purchase inexpensively and locally or that you can "borrow" from your own home. Sources for obtaining the materials presented for the activities are noted in Appendix B at the end of the book.

Montessori Practical Life skills are a wonderful addition to any program or home environment. Enrollment in a Montessori school does provide a wonderful education for children; however, for many children the reality is that such programs can be beyond their ability due to location, financial costs, and other such realities. Montessori Practical Life skills should be available for all children. This book will provide the information, examples, and ideas to implement these valuable activities into the homes and preschool programs of all children.

Practical Life in its essence is simple. It is based on the fact that children love to do what they see the grownups in their life doing. Watch as they want to "help" you do activities such as cook, fold clothes, and sweep the floor. These elements provide the basis of Practical Life. Simple activities which mimic the everyday things people do.

These activities are much more than play for young children. They teach important cognitive knowledge, developmental skills, fine motor skills, and concentration. Practical Life exercises require children to concentrate as they work hard to do the activities well. It is wonderful to observe children as they develop such skills while enjoying the process.

When using the Montessori philosophy, the work materials can be called activities and the process is called "work." This differs from more traditional programs which usually refer to children's materials as toys and the process is called play. I owned a "Montessori-Based" child care center and it was very common for the children to correct teachers or parents who called the materials toys. They would quickly let the grownups know that those items were activities not toys. Being a blended program, we also had toys for play time which were considered and used differently from the "activities" used for our "work" or lesson time.

Montessori is a method of teaching and there are many different educational components to the method. This book focuses on one of my favorite parts of the Montessori Method - the wonderful Practical Life activities. These activities can be fully integrated into a structured Montessori program. In addition, these same activities can bring great benefits when incorporated into traditional programs.

The wonderful benefits and activities of Practical Life can be useful in all early childhood environments. Home environments and child care centers can easily implement Montessori Practical Life lessons and activities into existing programs. These activities can be set up in a Montessori style with shelves dedicated to these Practical Life activities. This is a typical Montessori set up which allows children to choose from numerous Practical Life activities and it is a key component to the Montessori environment. Another option for parents or centers using more traditional curriculum is to use the Practical Life activities as centers and simply rotate the activities. This method doesn't provide the Montessori environment along with numerous choices in activities. It does, however, provide all of the benefits of the individual Practical Life activities and is a good option for implementing the activities into a traditional setting.

In this book, I will show you how simple materials can be put together to create wonderful activities for young children. These activities are not original, they are timeless and simple. Practical Life activities can be found throughout books, internet, and numerous other sources. This book puts together many activities which are divided into content areas and it compiles useful and creative Practical Life ideas into a form which is easy to use for parents and teachers working with small children. During busy days working with small children, it is easy to get in a rut and do the same activities over and over. It can be difficult to have the time to think about and research for more ideas to add to your Practical Life program. This book puts it all together so that you can simply look through the pages, gather a few basic materials, and easily add new activities to your Practical Life program. It is not comprehensive. It is intended to be an idea book that you can take and use to copy ideas as well as spark your imagination to create your own activities.

There are many ways to use the activities and extensions. Alternate ways of using activities are discussed in many areas. As you work with young children, you can easily recreate the activities in the book. In addition, you can use the ideas as a springboard for your own imagination. The options and ideas of Practical Life skills are unlimited! Join in the fun of creating your own Practical Life activities and watch the joy on the children's faces as they concentrate, learn, and "work."

All of the materials used in the book were either taken from my own home, purchased locally, or bought online through sources listed in the back of the book. The materials used were inexpensive and easily obtainable. The pictures were taken in my own home and without professional photography. This is "Montessori Made Easy" and it is a format that is obtainable for all teachers and parents. I hope this book provides many opportunities for teachers, parents, and young children to benefit from the wonderful applications of Montessori Practical Life by making it simple, easy, inexpensive, and obtainable. The book is designed to provide early childhood teachers and parents the basis to create their own Practical Life activities. References to gender, such as he or she, are used interchangeably throughout the book.

The book is not intended to be a complete source of Practical Life materials. The ideas are not original but instead timeless. Similar information can be found in many different resources. The book provides all of the time consuming research, information on how to put materials together, and many examples which are organized into chapters based on the skills and concepts of the materials. The book seeks to provide parents and teachers with a resource that can be easily accessible and usable so that the implementation of Practical Life lessons is quick and easy to construct. In addition, the book provides a resource for examples of materials and where specialty materials for Practical Life can be easily located at affordable prices.

These materials may be used exactly as presented or duplicated, and changed to meet individual needs. In addition, this idea book is created to open your imagination and provide a springboard to even more Practical Life activities for the children in your care. Take the ideas, use materials that are easily obtainable and inexpensive, and enjoy the process of creating wonderful materials for children's Practical Life lessons.

When utilizing Montessori materials in a home setting, select materials which are appropriate based on the developmental level of your own child. Be sure to supervise your child carefully as he works with those materials. When utilizing Montessori materials in a preschool or child care setting, be sure that you are complying with any regulations which are applicable to your school or child care center. Pay careful attention to age and developmental requirements of children. Provide only materials which are appropriate for the needs of the particular children in your care.

1

What is Practical Life?

Practical Life

Practical Life is in essence simple activities for children which emulate everyday activities. These simple activities should be purposeful and calm. They are done repetitively to build both concentration and skills in young children. Montessori Practical Life is generally designed for young children. These activities can be a part of early childhood for children as young as 12 months; provided the adult in charge takes care with safety concerns such as small pieces or adapts the activities to suit the ages of the very young children. The Practical Life exercises are very interesting and entertaining to younger children up until the age of three. As children get older and master the basic Practical Life skills, these are less appealing. Four and five year old children will also enjoy Practical Life activities, but will tend to choose them less often as these activities now are easier and no longer require the same level of focus and challenge that they once did. Practical Life can continue well after that age with the addition of more complicated skills embedded into your lessons. These more complex skills are easily considered part of older children's development as well. If you really consider the premise of Practical Life, children continue to learn everyday skills for many years. These skills would become more complex such as cooking skills, doing laundry for the family, washing, and putting up the dishes. These everyday skills are part of learning and growing with children

Benefits of Practical Life

The benefits of including Practical Life in the education of young children are extensive. These activities will help children fully develop their fine motor skills and increase their ability to concentrate as they focus on a particular Practical Life exercise. Children master these skills as they repeat the simple activities over and over again. The children are able to perfect their abilities by learning from trial and error. For instance, in a pouring activity, when the water continues to the top of the cup and spills over, the child learns that she needs to stop pouring sooner. While repeating the activities, the child is also learning to concentrate on a particular activity for an extended period of time.

Children also learn self-discipline as a part of Practical Life skills. This happens as children choose their activities, work with concentration, return activities to their appropriate place on the shelf, and care for their environment by keeping it clean and taking care of the materials. Self-confidence is another benefit of including Practical Life skills in a child's early education. Self-confidence is gained as children learn how to "do-it-themselves," while completing activities and repeating them until they have mastered the activities.

Basics of Practical Life

Practical Life activities are called "work" or "exercises." It is not called play. This distinction is noted as children want to do the "work" that they see grownups do. In addition, children learn that they enjoy "work" and it provides a positive perception of work in their eyes.

One key component of the materials used to create sets of Practical Life activities is that the materials should be real, rather than toys. Children enjoy working with the same materials that they see the grownups using. If possible, choose authentic materials to work with. This means items that are "real" but "child sized" so that the activities are easy for children to manipulate. This is especially true for the youngest children with very small hands. These real materials are almost endless. Create activity sets which utilize different colors, patterns, and textures. This creates a beautiful environment and adds interest for the child. Having several different pouring activities allows children to enjoy the activity more and learn how to pour from different containers. The interest is extended because even though the basics of the activity are the same, the child has a number of options to choose from and he will want to explore each one of the different sets of materials. The interest would not be the same if the materials looked exactly the same but simply came in different sizes. While selecting your materials, try to utilize a great deal of natural colored materials. This enhances the beauty and authenticity of the materials and provides that calm beautiful environment that is associated with a Montessori classroom and materials.

In a world of brightly colored, cheap, plastic toys; it is refreshing, natural, and authentic to minimize these materials in your Practical Life shelves. The natural materials such as wood bowls and straw baskets are more expensive than plastic spoons and bowls but it adds to the beauty and interest of the materials. In addition, utilize the sources at the back of the book for locating such materials which look authentic but are not breakable or expensive. You may find that you need to enhance your materials with some of the plastic and colorful materials in order to reduce costs and sometimes that is all that is available for the materials that you want. That is fine and sometimes the right choice. Just be sure to blend those bright colorful pieces into a shelf with many natural colored materials.

There are numerous sources for Montessori Practical Life materials which can be purchased in complete sets. These are often expensive. The materials don't need to be expensive. By purchasing a few child sized items and adding those to real materials that you already have around your house or child care center, you can create wonderful Practical Life activities for very little cost.

The Montessori methods often uses glass in activities. The origins of the method date back to 1907. The basis for using items which are breakable provide the real life understanding that items must be handled carefully or the child will experience the logical consequence – it breaks! Whether you choose to use real glass containers or not will depend on how and for whom you are creating your activities. If you are at home and working with your own child or children, you may choose to keep these traditional Montessori materials as a part of your Practical Life area. However, if you are creating materials for use in a group environment such as a child care center, then it is not recommended that you have glass materials readily available and accessible to the children. I did use "heavy and sturdy" glass materials on occasion in my own child care center; however, they were not left on open shelves. These materials were only pulled down on special occasions when a teacher could sit right with the children and carefully supervise each move. It isn't the logical consequence of breakage that is a concern. It is the potential for children being injured from that broken glass that must be carefully considered and prevented. Even when I used the glass under supervision, I chose not to ever use the more fragile forms of glass due to the potential for injury.

There are many materials available today that look very nice and look breakable but are actually plastic. These materials make wonderful additions to your Practical Life activities. You can find them easily at local discount stores, party stores, dollar stores, and restaurant supply stores. When choosing your materials, look for items in different colors and patterns. Choose items that are smaller, such as small plates and small scoops. Sources for obtaining these materials are listed in the back of the book. Other long-time elements of Practical Life exercises include cleaning skills using real cleaners such as polishing silver and shoes. Although these were historically used; utilizing cleaning products is not recommended due to the obvious hazard of a child ingesting a poisonous substance.

One final note on Practical Life skills is that these activities are about process not product. Children are actively doing the activities. For parents at home, you are well aware of what your child is learning through the activities. For teachers in schools and child care centers, it may be beneficial to send home notes of all of the wonderful activities that the children are working on to keep parents informed. In our modern world, it often seems if there isn't a piece of paper or an actual product, parents don't always realize that their children were busy working and learning during the day. Communication of the value and benefits of time spent in Practical Life activities is very important. It allows you to bring the parents into the understanding of what their child is doing, why it is important, and the long term benefits created through your Practical Life curriculum components.

Adding Practical Life exercises to your early childhood program provides wonderful benefits for children as they love the beauty; warm earth tones; interesting materials and textures; calm activities; concentration; building fine motor skills; and the joy of accomplishment. It's easy and inexpensive. Enjoy the process and watch the benefits as you fill your Practical Life shelves. Let's get started.

2

Environment and Presentation

Environment

The Montessori Practical Life environment provides a calm sense of order. It is based on a prepared environment. The materials are prepared and set out attractively to provide interest for the children. The children select materials from the shelf that they would like to work on and are allowed to concentrate on that work for as long as they would like to do so. This prepared environment, level of choice, and ability to concentrate without interruption provide a calm and pleasant learning environment. Parents who are new to the Montessori environment are often amazed by the level of calm and order as the children are self-motivated to work on and learn from materials in the environment.

Setting up a Practical Life area is easy. In order to provide your children with a Montessori Practical Life area, choose a shelf to display your materials. If your space allows, utilize a number of shelving units in your Montessori Practical Life area. Keep them all in one area in order to create a specific area for completing the Practical Life activities. Organize your space by types of materials; such as one shelf for pouring and spooning activities; another shelf for cleaning materials; and another shelf for art and design materials. In a Montessori format, the materials are laid out on a shelf and the each child is allowed to choose the particular activity that he wants to work with. The child should be allowed to work with the materials for as long as he wants; repeating and perfecting the skills for the activity. Once the child is through with working on that particular activity, he should put it back into the basket or tray neatly and return the materials to the shelf. He may then choose another activity to work on.

Shelf Materials

If you are setting up a Practical Life area in a traditional school or child care center you may have space limitations as you try to create an area for Practical Life among your other classroom needs. Likewise, if you are working out of your home, creating a dedicated space can be challenging. In such cases, you can create a single shelf of materials and rotate the items. If you like the idea of a more traditional program with "learning centers" rather than shelves of open materials, you can set up your Practical Life activities as centers. You will have fewer options for children to choose from at one time. This provides a very different type of environment from the Montessori classroom layout; however, it will allow you to utilize the wonderful Practical Life activities within the scope of your own home-based learning design, the traditional school classroom model, and even the learning center model which is very popular in child care centers.

This is an example of a shelving unit with activities laid out in complete sets. It shows a variety of activities, colors, textures, and containers displayed simply and attractively. The use of trays, baskets, and wooden boxes create a means to contain all of the materials for activities as well as a way to easily carry the materials to a mat or table.

In the Montessori environment, each activity has a specific place on the shelf. Children are taught to pay attention to where each activity belongs. As a child chooses an activity to work with, he should pay attention to where it belongs and be sure to return it to the correct place when he is done.

Some Practical Life materials in the book are perfect for shelf materials. These are the materials that can sit on a shelf; be used by a child; and then be returned to the shelf for the next child to use. These are materials that are relatively neat, dry, and do not need replenishing on a regular basis. Throughout the book, there are also materials which may be placed on a shelf but at the teacher or parent's option, may be better suited for a center type area. These would be materials which require very careful supervision or frequent replacement of materials. Examples of these Practical Life materials include working with real food, exercises that include pouring colored water, and exercises that may use small pieces or breakable materials. When including these types of materials in your Practical Life lessons, it is often beneficial to limit these to only one or two at a time. These can be special and exciting activities that are set out for only a day or a week and then another activity replaces them for the next time frame.

Another key component to learning in a Montessori environment is that children are allowed to "choose their work" and keep it as long as they would like to work on it. This allows children to concentrate. In the purest sense, children are not to be interrupted while they are working as this breaks their concentration. The Montessori environment is a structured environment; however, it is a structure which supports the individual child's freedom to choose what he wants to work with, how long he wants to work on it, and decide when to put the activity away.

Mats, Tables, and Floor Space

Mats, tables, and open floor space are another key component of the Montessori classroom. Some activities are best worked with on tables; other activities are best completed on mats. In addition, the floor should contain ample open space in order to provide room for group time as well as for spreading mats on the floor to complete activities.

In a classroom setting, you will want to have some child sized tables for children to use while working on Practical Life activities such as pouring and scooping. When choosing tables for your Montessori Practical Life area, wood or natural colored tables are preferable. These will enhance the beauty and appearance of your Montessori environment.

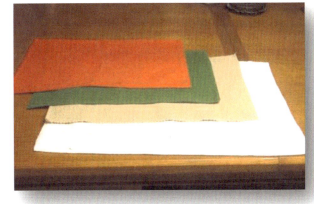

In a home environment, you may choose to have children simply sit at your kitchen table. Just make sure that your child is sitting up high enough (using a booster seat if necessary) to be able to have a comfortable range of motion and be able to complete activities with accuracy. Mats can be utilized equally well in both classroom and home environments. Mats have a special purpose as they designate a child's space. Children should place their mats on the floor and spread them out neatly. Teach the children to use the mats as an important space. Walk around mats. Never step on top of mats. Children should not touch or take things from someone else's mat. This is a special place designated for one child and his materials.

Mats for Montessori activities can be purchased online and through Montessori catalogs. These can be expensive. A good alternative to such purchases is to look at your local discount store for appropriate items which can be used as Montessori mats. If you are choosing a mat for a child or children in your home, then one mat per child should be sufficient for your needs. If you are choosing mats for a classroom of children, then it is a good idea to purchase mats in two or three different sizes. Smaller mats are good for small activities which are easily completed on the floor. These are easier for smaller children to handle and small mats will also take up less floor space. Larger mats are a good choice for activities which can take up a significant amount of room.

Good choices for affordable mats include small floor rugs, bathroom rugs, and accent rugs. For small mats, placemats are a good choice. When choosing your mats, look for simple mats in a solid color. White, off white, and earth tones are good color choices. Other colors can be utilized as well. The solid color is important because it is basic, and it makes it easy for small children to find all of the pieces to an activity on these mats. When a mat has many colors, sometimes activity pieces are harder to see and it also creates a very "busy" background for concentration. It is also best to look for mats made of materials that can be laundered. This is especially important in group environments to clean stains, and sanitize materials used repeatedly by multiple children.

Traditional storage of mats in the Montessori environment includes rolling up the mats; therefore, it is best to choose mats that can be easily rolled up as shown in the example. These mats can be stored in attractive straw baskets to continue the natural look of your Montessori environment.

The mat should be used by the child just as a table would be used. Teaching a child to use a mat as a workspace means demonstrating how to choose a mat from the storage basket; take it to the work area; lay it on the floor; unroll the mat on the floor; and smooth out the wrinkles until it is completely flat. Next, the Practical Life activity should be chosen from the shelf and carried to the mat. Place the work on the mat and then sit on the floor beside the mat. The mat provides a place for the materials and a designated work space for the child. The child should not sit on the mat.

This designated space provides not only a comfortable place for children to work but the children understand that they don't have to worry about another child taking their things when they get up for a restroom break, snack or other reason. This was often one of the first things that concerned children when they began classes at my Montessori preschool. Children who came from more traditional child care settings were often concerned about their things being taken by another child if they left their mat for a moment. They were comforted in the structure and atmosphere of a classroom which respects each individual's space and learning opportunities.

In a classroom setting, often it is the parents who need to be educated about the use of mats. It is very common for parents to walk through a classroom where children are working and step on numerous mats as they cross the floor. Advise your parents on the purpose of the mats and the importance of respecting the materials and space.

Presentation

Presentation is an important part of the education experience in the Montessori Method. Each activity is presented prior to children using it. The correct way to use the materials is demonstrated to the children. Presentations can be made to an entire class of children at one time, to a small group of children, or to an individual child. The setting, particular Practical Life exercise, and circumstances determine which is best. Be sure to pay special attention to which hand is dominant for each child when providing the presentation of how to complete activities. If the child is left handed and the teacher is right handed, it is important to show the child how to complete the activity based on their left hand being the dominant hand.

In the beginning of the school year or home lessons, take the time to teach your children the basic skills. These basic skills include teaching your children how to roll up their mats and how to store them as a part of taking care of their environment. Other basic skills to include in early lessons are pushing their chairs in when getting up from a table, putting materials back in the correct place, cleaning up after themselves, as well as keeping their shelves and activities neat and clean.

Begin each new activity with a demonstration. When demonstrating an activity, the teacher should start by going to the shelf of materials and selecting the new material. Pick up and carry the materials to the mat or table where the activity will be used. While doing this, the teacher is demonstrating how the children are to handle and carry the materials. Set the activity down on the mat or table and go through the steps of how the materials should be used. As a general rule, all material processes should move from left to right. This is based on the process of preparing for reading where words are read from left to right.

Tell the children in detail such things as how to hold the materials, and exactly how to complete each step of the activity. You can have the children take a turn at trying out the activity, which is fun for them. New materials to work with are very exciting and everyone wants to give them a try. When you are presenting to a number of children, allowing each child an opportunity to try the new materials has significant benefits. This method will help the children learn how to use the activity, as well as, help them have a little more patience as they wait for their turn, once the materials are on the shelf.

Materials are set on the shelf and each Practical Life activity is unique. For example, there may be several pouring activities but each one would include different materials and even slightly different skills as demonstrated in the different pouring activities in Chapter 4. Children at times will need to wait for someone to complete an activity and place it back on the shelf before they get a turn with that particular activity. This is important as it teaches patience. There should be plenty of materials to choose from but at times children will need to be patient before their favorite one is available.

Once the demonstration is complete, the teacher should put the activity back in its proper place on the shelf. Remind the children to put the set back where it came from. If you are using the materials in a more contemporary "learning center" based classroom, then the presentation should be completed at the center. The teacher should then reinforce that all of the materials for the center are to stay in that particular area and be kept together.

Many of the activities also include extensions. These are just ways to enhance the skills and interest by using different materials. Some of the extensions increase the skill levels by adding different work materials or methods, while other extensions simply add interest by utilizing different materials when practicing the same skills. As you further develop your Practical Life skills use these concepts to develop more activities and increase interest as your child practices skills using different materials and methods.

3
Scooping and Transferring

Materials for Scooping and Transferring

The materials used to scoop and transfer are simple and inexpensive. Many are probably already in your pantry.

Examples of materials which can be utilized in these Practical Life exercises include:

- Dried Beans
- Dried Peas
- Raw Rice
- Dried Pasta
- Cornmeal
- Grits
- Cream of Wheat

These materials come in many different varieties and range from large red beans, to black eyed peas, and even tiny lentils. There is a great deal of fun and interest in these basic materials. A favorite of these is the 9 Bean Soup which has a fun variety of sizes and shapes. This is also good for sorting skills as well as transferring exercises.

Dried pasta also comes in many fun shapes and sizes from very tiny shapes, which can be ladled or scooped, to large pieces which can utilize tongs and pinching skills to transfer. The variety adds interest. When you include multiple types of scooping and transferring activities on your Practical Life shelves it adds a great deal of fun and interest by using different colors, shapes, and sizes. In addition, the different sizes and shapes will require further refinement of the fine motor skills used during these Practical Life exercises.

Many different tools can also be used in the transferring of these basic materials. The tools used should vary based on the materials used; such as using a tiny spoon for transferring salt or very small grains; utilizing a mustard spoon for transferring individual beans or peas; and using a child sized ladle on fine materials for perfecting the scooping motion; and using tongs for practicing pinching skills and through transferring individual pieces of pasta. The grains, dried peas, and dried beans can all be purchased inexpensively at your local grocery store. The tiny tools for transferring Practical Life exercises can be purchased at Montessori supply stores. The resource information is found in Appendix B.

Spooning Dry Beans

Materials Needed

- ❖ 9 Bean Soup / or Other Dry Beans
- ❖ Small Straw Baskets / or Other Small Containers
- ❖ Tiny Wood Spoon
- ❖ Presentation Tray to Hold and Display Materials

Presentation and Activity:

Work from left to right. Begin with the beans in a basket on the left and the empty basket on the right, as shown in the example. Pick up a few beans with the spoon and transfer them into the second basket. Repeat until all of the beans have been transferred. Once the activity has been completed, use the spoon to transfer the beans back into the first basket. Repeat the activity as desired.

Spooning Dry Beans Extensions

The following activities are extensions of spooning dry beans. These allow additional practice along with increased levels of skills as each activity uses slightly different materials and skills. Using different materials both as part of your display and actual work (such as different types of utensils used to transfer) creates additional interest in the activities and encourages repetition in practice. In a center, these extensions allow even more sets of materials on your shelves for greater access to these activities by all of the children.

Extension 1

Materials Needed

- ❖ 9 Bean Soup / or Other Dry Beans
- ❖ Display Bowl
- ❖ Condiment Cups
- ❖ Child Size Stainless Steel Scoop

Presentation and Activity:

Scoop up several beans at one time with the mini scoop and transfer them into the different cups. Repeat until all of the beans have been transferred. Once the activity is complete, pour the beans from the condiment cups, back into the larger bowl. Then the activity can be repeated if desired.

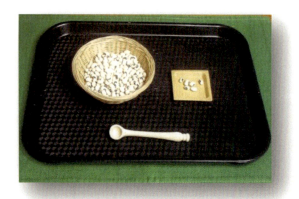

Extension 2

This extension uses the addition of a mustard spoon. This tiny spoon is designed to focus on picking up one bean at a time. This allows the child to work toward greater skill and concentration. Using only one type of bean or pea, it creates a more simplistic activity. In this activity, the child can focus fully on the process rather than the different colors and textures.

Extension 3

This extension uses the mustard spoon and 9 Bean Soup mix. The activity can be utilized to extend the skills by sorting different types of beans into individual condiment cups. Additional extensions can include sorting by size and color.

Spooning Rice with a Ladle

Materials Needed

- ❖ Serving Dish or Tray
- ❖ Two Small Bowls
- ❖ Dry Rice
- ❖ Child Size Ladle

Presentation and Activity:

Pick up a ladle full of rice and transfer it to the second bowl. Repeat until all of the rice has been transferred. After all of the rice is transferred to the bowl on the right, using the ladle, transfer the rice back into the bowl on the left. Then the activity can be repeated if desired.

Extension

This extension uses a different grain, such as dried peas or lintels, it is a simple extension just using a different form of grain and changing the type of containers. This creates an additional interest as well as utilizing an extension of skills due to the different grain used and the different shape of the containers.

Mixing and Sifting

Materials Needed

- ❖ Cornmeal
- ❖ Large Dry Beans
- ❖ Small Mixing Bowl
- ❖ Condiment Cup or Very Small Bowl
- ❖ Spoon
- ❖ Very Small Wire Strainer

Presentation and Activity:

Mix the beans into the cornmeal using the spoon. Next, use strainer to sift the beans out of the cornmeal and place them into the smaller bowl on the left. When all of the beans have been sifted out, they can be poured back into the cornmeal and the process repeated.

Transferring Dry Pasta

Materials Needed
- ❖ Dry Macaroni
- ❖ Small Wooden Spoon
- ❖ Small Sauce Pan
- ❖ Small Serving Bowls
- ❖ Demonstration Tray

Presentation and Activity:

Stir the dry pasta and then spoon it into the serving bowls. After it is complete, the pasta should be poured back into the pot so that the activity can be repeated. This is a fun activity as children will really relate to using a real sauce pan and can pretend to make one of their favorite foods.

Extensions

This extension uses tri-colored rotini pasta. It requires a somewhat different skill as the child uses a spoon to transfer these noodles due to their longer size and different shape. This provides a fun shape and the addition of color.

This extension can be adapted in numerous ways. There are many shapes of pasta which can be used to create interest and requiring slightly different skills to manipulate. This Practical Life activity can also be varied by using different tools for scooping pasta such as ladles, and spoons with a different surface area. Varying the display materials also creates additional interest in the activity.

Combining Transferring and Sorting Skills

These skills take transferring one step further into the area of sorting. This sorting is utilized in Montessori lessons under the curriculum area of sensorial activities. The concept of sorting is also an early math skill which is readily utilized in traditional education settings, so these activities provide the benefits of both fine motor as well as early academic processing skills.

Transferring and Sorting Two Types of Beans

Materials Needed

- ❖ Medium Size Display Bowl
- ❖ Two Small Containers
- ❖ Mini-Ladle or Spoon
- ❖ Two Different Types of Beans or Other Grains
- ❖ Display Tray

Presentation and Activity:

Use the ladle to scoop up the beans. Push some of the like kinds of beans together with the ladle. Then using a small scooping motion, pick up several of the black eyed peas and transfer them into one of the small bowls. Next, repeat the process but this time scoop up several of the red beans and transfer those into the second small bowl. Repeat the process until all of the beans and peas have been sorted into the smaller bowls. Then, pick up the small bowls and pour the contents back into the larger container. Use the ladle to mix the beans and peas together. The materials are now ready to repeat the process or set the tray back on the shelf for another child to use.

Transferring and Sorting Beans Extensions

Extension 1

This extension uses a very small wooden spoon to sort and transfer numerous types of beans from a 9 Bean Soup mix. An ice tray makes an easy and effective sorting container.

This can also be utilized as an early math activity by specifying a number for each ice cube space and having the child place the correct number of beans into that space. For example, place one bean in the first opening, two beans in the second opening, three in the third opening, and continue the process.

Extension 2

This extension uses a paint pallet and a wooden mustard spoon. The paint pallet makes an interesting sorter for different types of grains. The example shows 9 Bean Soup as the grains for sorting in this extension.

Extension 3

This extension uses the tri-colored rotini pasta. It utilizes three bowls and tiny tongs. This activity allows the child to utilize different fine motor skills as the transferring is done with tongs. In addition, the child can sort the pasta into the three different bowls using each bowl for a single color of pasta.

Using Real Food in Practical Life

The Practical Life activities in this section include using real food. Just as using real dishes, flatware, and other material provides a greater interest and authenticity for children, using real food in activities creates more of a sense of "real" life skills for children. These particular activities are designed as shelf materials rather than food that is intended to be eaten. With this in mind, these activities require more preparation for the teacher as the foods used will need to be replaced each day and the materials cleaned.

Many of these activities do have the potential to be combined with snack time if desired. There are more activities in Chapter 4 and Chapter 5 which include utilizing Practical Life skills in creating drinks and food that the children can include in their snacks or meals. Be sure to carefully monitor the activities used here to prevent cross contamination of foods.

These particular activities, when used as shelf materials or combined with snacks and meals will require more preparation than typical shelf materials. Therefore, it is best to limit the number of these activities to only one or two on any single day.

Transferring Dry Food

Materials Needed

- ❖ Medium Size Display Bowl
- ❖ Smaller Bowl or Dish
- ❖ Child Size Tongs
- ❖ Cheese Puffs
- ❖ Display Tray

Presentation and Activity:

Use the tongs to carefully pick up and transfer each cheese puff to the small bowl. The transfer of the real foods shown in this section requires an increased level of concentration and fine motor skills in order to avoid dropping or damaging the food.

Extension 1

This extension utilizes crackers which are transferred using full size tongs. The full size tongs along with larger flat crackers provide the opportunity for a different technique for the child to master.

Extension 2

This extension utilizes dry cereal which is transferred using a child size ladle. The addition of a ladle and small cereal creates another technique for transfer.

Extension 3

Caution: Popcorn can pose a choking hazard for very young children. This activity is best for children ages 3 and up. Even though the popcorn may not be intended for eating, for some children the temptation will be hard to resist.

This extension uses popcorn which is transferred using small tongs. Using tongs reinforces the pinching skills that are important to many developmental applications including learning to write.

Turning Dry Food

Materials Needed

- Small Lightweight Skillet
- Child Size Spatula
- Piece of French Toast or Other Bread
- Display Tray

Presentation and Activity:

Take the turner in the dominant hand. Hold the skillet steady by the handle with the other hand. Slide the turner under the piece of toast and turn it over. It is fun to pretend to cook with real materials while learning this skill.

Extensions

This extension utilizes a piece of bread cut into quarters and the addition of two small plates. The child can then utilize the skills of both turning along with transferring the "cooked" food to the serving plates.

This Practical Life activity can be utilized as a shelf activity without real food by simply replacing the toast with flat bean bags. This is not as authentic but it provides a practical daily use for the activity.

Transferring Canned Vegetables

Materials Needed

- ❖ Small to Medium Size Bowl
- ❖ Two Very Small Size Bowls
- ❖ Teaspoon
- ❖ One Can of Corn
- ❖ Display Tray

Presentation and Activity:

Lift the lid off of the bowl and set it on the tray. Take the spoon in the dominant hand and scoop some corn into it. Transfer the corn to one of the small bowls and turn the spoon to the side and let the corn fall into the bowl. Continue the process until all of the corn has been transferred to the small bowls. The corn may be poured from the small bowls back into the serving bowl as part of the Practical Life exercise. These activities using canned food are fun and have a very authentic feel for the child; however, using them can be messy.

These activities using real food can also be combined with a lunch or snack. In this case, the child would be able to eat the corn that he spooned into the bowl.

Extension 1

This activity utilizes the same concepts with the substitution of green beans for corn. Green beans are more challenging to spoon due to their long shape.

Extension 2

This extension uses a can of green beans and a small "seafood fork." This activity presents a different challenge as the child needs to be able to transfer the green beans with the fork without tearing them. It requires an added level of fine motor skills and concentration.

Transferring and Stirring Canned Vegetables

Materials Needed

- ❖ Small Saucepan
- ❖ Child Size Wooden Spoon
- ❖ Small Bowl
- ❖ Display Tray

Presentation and Activity:

Use the wooden spoon to carefully stir the beans without tearing them. This requires a gentle motion. After stirring and pretending to cook, transfer the green beans to the bowl using the wooden spoon.

Extensions

This activity uses two types of vegetables. The object is to carefully mix the two together such as the motion of making a soup. The skills include pouring from the small bowls and mixing the vegetable.

If you want to add water, you could further extend the activity by incorporating pouring skills and the children could enjoy the activity while pretending to make vegetable soup.

4

Pouring and Transferring

Pouring Liquids

Water and colored water can be shelf materials – just make sure to replace those regularly and keep towels nearby so that children can learn to clean up their spills.

Colored water can be mixed easily using food colors. This is a good project to have the child complete with you. It is a fun experiential activity to see how adding a drop of food coloring changes the color of the water. Be aware that depending on the food coloring used and the amount of color added, spills of colored water may stain some surfaces including carpets.

The child will spill water during the practice of pouring liquids. It is normal and should be expected. This is where the value of authentic materials really comes into play. Pretending to pour doesn't create the need to understand how the skills must be adjusted. If the child misses the container; overflows the cup; pours to fast; or other such mistakes; then, he will understand the need to adjust his pouring skills.

Each activity in the pouring section includes a tray to catch most spills. It should catch most of the water but be prepared for spills which go beyond the container. You may want to set up a special area just for pouring activities. When using colored water, take extra care to set the activities over a hard floor or place a water proof covering (such as a plastic table cloth or shower curtain) over carpets as these may create stains.

Pouring Liquids

Materials Needed

- ❖ Teapot
- ❖ Teacup
- ❖ Tray

Presentation and Activity:

Hold the teapot handle with the dominant hand and place the other hand under the spout to provide support and control. Carefully position the spout over the tea cup and pour the water into the cup until it is full then set the tea cup back down. Open the lid on the teapot. Then pick up the cup and slowly pour the water back into the teapot. The activity can then be repeated.

Extension 1

This extension uses a small plastic pitcher and tiny 5 oz juice cups. The pitcher is held in the same manner as the teapot when pouring.

Extension 2

This extension uses a small stainless steel creamer and demitasse espresso cups for pouring water. This technique is the same as in the other pouring exercises. This extension allows the child another opportunity to work with materials that are different in size and shape.

Extension 3

This extension incorporates a syrup pitcher and colored water into the pouring exercises. Colored water is made by simply adding food color to your water. You can make the colored water as dark or as light as your would like. Just keep in mind that darker colored water will be more likely to stain surfaces.

Demonstrate the activity by placing your hand in the same position as in the other pouring exercises. Next, show the child how to press the handle on the lid to open the spout. After opening the spout, use two hands to pour the colored water into the condiment cups.

Extension 4

This extension includes using a pitcher from an oil and vinegar salad set, condiment cups, and colored water. Carefully remove the lid, place it on the display tray, and then place your hands on the pitcher just as in the other pouring exercises.

Extension 5

This extension uses a beautiful child size sake set for pouring. It creates a visual interest that the child will enjoy and it adds the addition of the one handed pouring skill. Demonstrate how to pour water by wrapping the dominant hand around the pitcher and fill the tiny sake cups using a one hand pouring technique.

Pouring Grains

Materials Needed

- Very Small Grains (Such as Rice or Lentils)
- Plastic Pitcher
- Tiny Plastic Cups
- Display Tray

Presentation and Activity:

Wrap the fingers of the dominant hand around the handle of the pitcher. Lift the pitcher and place the spout over one of the bowls. Gently pour the grains into the bowl. When the bowl is full, repeat the process with the second bowl. After both bowls are full, lift one of the bowls up and pour the grains back into the pitcher. Repeat with the second bowl. The activity is then ready to be repeated.

Grain pouring is a great activity to leave out on your shelves. The materials are shelf stable and simply need to be refilled when the level of material decreases significantly from spills.

Plastic pitchers that look like glass are a really nice addition to your Practical Life area. These materials look authentic and provide a great interest to the child while at the same time keeping the child free from the possibility of breaking glass.

Extensions

The process of pouring grains can be incorporated into many other pouring materials that were used in the pouring liquids exercises. The only difference is that the opening of the pitcher must be wide enough to accommodate the grains used. Enjoy creating pouring grain exercises and incorporate different varieties of pitchers as well as different fine grains, such as cornmeal cream, cream of wheat, grits, and others.

Transferring Liquids

The transfer of liquids creates a new skill for the child. This method does not pour liquids but uses utensils to transfer them into other containers. It develops the skills of scooping, ladling, and spooning as the child learns to manipulate these objects. It is a fun skill as children can pretend to ladle soup into a bowl just as they see the adults around them do.

The first examples of transferring liquids make wonderful activities to leave out on your Practical Life shelf. Just as with the activities involving pouring water, the water needs to be replaced daily. In addition, it is recommended that you create an area that children will use when completing these exercises involving water. This area should be: appropriate to contain spills; keep the wet spills and clean ups away from your other shelf materials; and have towels available.

The materials can be shelved in this area or you may choose to place them on the shelves with the other materials; simply instruct children where to work on these activities since they include using water. Be sure to complete your presentations of these materials in the area that you want the children to work on them.

Some of the extensions which include colored water and adding ingredients to the water will require preparation daily. These activities would generally not be included in your shelf materials which are left out from day to day, but would be special activities which are presented on particular days. These activities would generally be limited to one activity per day or even just one activity chosen on special days since they require additional preparation and clean up each time they are used.

The final activities presented in the chapter include the preparation of drinks, which are intended to be consumed during a snack or even at a meal time. Combining a Practical Life skill, which includes making a real drink that they can consume, is very exciting for children. It is special because each activity is only done once and it is definitely authentic because it is real. There are few activities that children enjoy more than participating in the preparation of drinks and food that they are then able to enjoy.

Transferring Water

Materials Needed

- ❖ Small to Medium Bowl
- ❖ Two Smaller Bowls
- ❖ Child Size Ladle
- ❖ Water
- ❖ Display Tray

Presentation and Activity:

This is a basic activity which utilizes a small rice bowl and two smaller individual bowls. The ladle is used to transfer water into the smaller bowls. If you have a lidded bowl, you have added another degree of interest. Demonstrate the activity by opening the lid and placing it on the tray or table. Show the child how to carefully dip the ladle into the bowl and raise it straight up so that the water stays in the ladle. Next, carefully transfer the water to the smaller bowls without spilling. After the activity is complete, demonstrate how to pour the water back into the larger bowl and have the child repeat the activity.

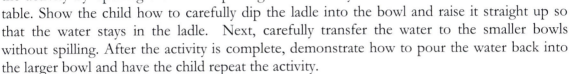

Extension 1

This extension uses a Chinese soup spoon to transfer liquid to smaller bowls. Yellow food coloring was added to make the water look like soup. Adding color to the water is optional but it does increase the authenticity of the exercise and the interest of the children.

Demonstrate how to transfer water from the medium size bowl to the small bowls using the spoon. Have the child complete the activity and then demonstrate how to pour the water from the small bowls back into the medium size bowl so that the activity can be repeated.

Extension 2

This extension uses a plastic baster to transfer water from a small bowl into condiment cups. The activity uses a pinching skill to draw water up into the device and hold it. Then it is transferred to the top of the condiment cups. As the pinching grip is released, the water flows into the small cups. It creates a fun extension which utilizes that very important pinching skill. An eye dropper can also be used if available, the basters are easier to find and readily available in the kitchen section of discounts stores.

Extensions Requiring Daily Replacements

The following extensions involve addition preparation and will require being cleaned up and resupplied each day; however, the additions included here create a fun variation to the activities. These can be intermittently used in order to create extensions and retain the children's interest in these transferring activities over time.

Extension 3

This extension takes the basic transfer from spooning just liquids while adding the simple touch of an additional ingredient such as rice. It adds interest and extends the practice into a new activity. Children can stir the bowl of colored water, spoon the rice and liquid into the bowls, and pretend that they are serving soup.

Extension 4

This is another possibility to extend the transfer of liquids through creating a new activity. This activity utilizes the same concepts as the one in Extension 3. The only differences are incorporating cereal that will float instead of rice and using a ladle rather than a soup spoon.

Preparing and Pouring a Drink

Materials Needed

- ❖ Small Child Sized Pitcher
- ❖ Two Small Cups
- ❖ Milk
- ❖ Display Tray

Presentation and Activity:

This first example is among the most simplistic. It is simply the activity of pouring. Demonstrate for the child how to hold the pitcher and pour. After demonstrating how to pour, place the child's dominant hand on the side with the handle and wrap the fingers around the handle. Place the child's other hand under the spout to guide the pouring into the small cups. For children who are just beginning to master the pouring skill, the pitcher should only be filled with a small amount of milk. More milk inside the pitcher creates a heavier pitcher which is more difficult for small children to manage successfully. As the children master the task, the pitcher can be filled more.

After the child has filled his cup, then he may drink the milk or take it to his table to be consumed with his other food.

Extension 1: Preparing and Pouring Chocolate Milk

This extension allows children to prepare one of their favorite drinks – chocolate milk. The child should be provided with a demonstration to understand how to squeeze the chocolate syrup into the pitcher, how much chocolate syrup to use, and finally how to stir the chocolate milk to mix it. After completing the process to prepare the chocolate milk, the child is now able to use her pouring skills to transfer the milk into a prepared cup.

Extension 2: Making Fresh Lemonade

Making lemonade is a fun application of preparing and pouring a drink. Prepare a tray with all of the necessary ingredients which are ready for the child to use. This includes a pitcher of cold water (or ice water), a manual juicer, lemons (already cut for the child), a small bowl of sugar, and a spoon for stirring. Demonstrate how to make the lemonade. Include the processes of: squeezing the lemons; pouring the lemon juice into the pitcher; spooning in the sugar; and stirring the lemonade. Then allow the child to make her own lemonade. After the drink is complete, have the child pour the lemonade into a child sized cup.

The activity should utilize a very small pitcher which is easily handled by a child. In addition, just as in the other examples, care should be taken to only fill the pitcher to a volume that is appropriate for the individual child completing the activity.

Extension 3: Fresh Squeezed Orange Juice

This activity is simple and yet it provides practice in a number of fine motor skills in order to make this delicious drink. The juicer shown in this example provides the child with a juicer which the child squeezes in order to create the juice. This activity could also be used with any other form of manual juicer such as the one shown in Extension 2. It requires fine motor skill, strength, and coordination in order to squeeze the juice out into the pitcher. The juice could also be squeezed directly into the cup. If you are using the juicer style shown in Extension 2, it would be a more simplistic activity since the juice is simply retained in the bottom of the bowl. The juicer used should be appropriate for the age of the child completing the activity.

Extension 4: Preparing and Pouring a Drink

This extension allows children to mix their own juice drink. It includes using a juice such as pineapple juice (shown here) and mixing it with carbonated water. This activity includes pouring skills along with the practical lessons of pouring slowly when serving carbonated drinks and understanding how much more room is used when the bubbles rise out of this type of drink.

Extension 5: More Materials and Ideas

This extension provides additional ideas to enhance the pouring activities. The use of a salad cruet makes a great pouring activity for small children. It is small and due to its unique shape and characteristics, it requires different skills. This activity requires the child to remove the sealed lid prior to pouring. It also requires a slightly different skill due to the shape of the bottle. By providing different opportunities for practice, the child learns how to adapt basic skills and increases both practice time and interest in the pouring activity. The tiny espresso cups also demonstrate one more possible way to utilize different materials in these Practical Life activities. As with all of the activities, use your imagination and what is readily available to create and enhance your Practical Life activities.

If the materials are breakable, take care in selecting whether or not the activity is appropriate for the child or children. As always, what is appropriate for a single adult and a child may not be a good choice in a child care center.

Extension 6: Making Ice Cubes

Making ice cubes is another Practical Life activity with real authenticity. It requires more advanced fine motor skills than the basic pouring activities. This is a good activity to add for children who have mastered the basic pouring skills.

Even more ideas and extension for ice cubes would include things like making colored ice cubes which are fun when put into water or other clear beverages. Flavored ice cubes could be made by pouring prepared lemonade, orange juice, or other drinks into the trays. The ice trays can be turned into ice pops by adding a sheet of plastic over the top and placing toothpicks or popsicle sticks through the plastic and into the trays.

5
Sifting and Straining

Straining

Materials Needed

- ❖ Medium or Small Bowl
- ❖ One Very Small Bowl or Cup
- ❖ Child Size Strainer
- ❖ Dry Beans, Peas, or Rice
- ❖ Water
- ❖ Display Tray

Presentation and Activity:

This is an activity which utilizes a small bowl filled with dry beans and water. Any variety of dry beans will work. The child will use the tiny strainer to master a scooping motion to retrieve the beans from the water and transfer them into the smaller container.

After the activity is complete, demonstrate how to put the beans back into the larger bowl so that the activity can be repeated.

Note: Activities such as this which utilize water along with other materials will require cleaning up and replenishing the supplies each day. These are best set up each day or as a special activity and not necessarily used as "shelf materials" which are left out each day.

Sifting

Materials Needed

- ❖ Medium or Small Bowl Filled with Flour or Cornmeal
- ❖ One Very Small Bowl or Cup with Lentils (or Other Small Grains)
- ❖ Child Size Strainer
- ❖ Child Size Wooden Spoon
- ❖ Display Tray

Presentation and Activity:

This activity utilizes several skills. The activity begins by pouring the lentils into the flour. The lentils are then stirred into the flour. Next, the strainer is used to sift the lentils back out of the flour. The child can then use a gently back and forth motion to sift the extra flour out of the strainer. Finally, the lentils can be poured back into the small cup. The activity can be repeated for as long as the child would like.

Notes: Anytime flour or cornmeal is used work can become very messy. The activity will likely require cleaning on a daily basis. However, it is appropriate as a shelf activity since all of the ingredients are dry and will not deteriorate if left out.

6

Food Preparation

Food Preparation

Caution: As always when preparing a food activity, make sure that the particular foods chosen are appropriate for the ages of the children who may be eating them and do not pose choking hazards. In addition, make sure that you are aware of any food allergies for the children in your care and make appropriate substitutions so that the children do not come into contact with such foods.

Grating Cheese

Caution: This activity requires careful supervision to avoid children's fingers being cut with the grater. In addition, be sure to replace the block of cheese well before it is small enough to create a hazard of children accidently grating their fingers rather than the cheese.

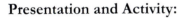

Materials Needed

- Small Hand Grater
- A Block of Mozzarella Cheese
- Display Tray
- Recommended: Bread, Noodles, or Other Food (to Put the Cheese on When the Activity is Complete)

Presentation and Activity:

Hold the cheese at a 90 degree angle against the top holes of the grater. Put gentle pressure on the cheese as you slide it down the grater. Repeat the motion from top to bottom.

Grating is a basic food preparation skill. It requires the specific movement from higher to lower and requires the child to apply the appropriate amount of pressure. Other cheeses may be used but mozzarella is recommended because it is soft and shreds easily for small children. This is a fun activity; especially when the end result is cheese can be eaten.

Slicing Cheese

Materials Needed

- Small Cheese Slicer or Blunt Knife
- A Single Child Size Block of Cheese
- Crackers
- Individual Serving Plate

Presentation and Activity:

Take the cheese slicer and place it on top of the cheese block. With the point down, push down and slice off a piece of cheese. Place the slice of cheese on the cracker. Repeat and enjoy this activity and those that follow as part of a snack.

Buttering a Roll

Materials Needed

- ❖ Roll (Sliced in Half)
- ❖ A Single Softened Pat of Butter
- ❖ Small Butter Spreader or Blunt Knife
- ❖ Individual Serving Plate

Presentation and Activity:

Demonstrate for the child how to open the sliced roll. Pick up the butter with the blade of the knife. Spread the butter over the roll gently without tearing the bread. It sounds like a simple activity but for very young children, this activity can be challenging at first. Children often have difficulty spreading butter without tearing up the bread. Combine the activity with snack time for a delicious and authentic experience.

Additional applications for this activity include spreading butter over a slice of bread, toast or a muffin; spreading cream cheese on a bagel; spreading jelly over a piece of toast; and making a peanut butter sandwich. There are many options to practice these skills and utilize this activity. These are just suggestions to get you started.

Sifting Powdered Sugar On French Toast

Materials Needed

- ❖ French Toast
- ❖ A Small Bowl of Powdered Sugar
- ❖ Small Sifter
- ❖ Serving Plate
- ❖ Display Tray

Presentation and Activity:

Demonstrate for the child how to scoop up some powdered sugar into the sifter. Next carefully sprinkle the sugar over the French toast. Have the child take the plate to the dining table and enjoy.

French toast could be made ahead in preparation for the activity or simply purchase frozen French toast from the grocery store and warm it up in a toaster or microwave. The toast should be allowed to cool down prior to the activity to avoid being too hot for children.

This activity is set up as an activity that is prepared in one area and moved to another area for eating. The fork, possibly a blunt knife, and drink would then be available at the table where the snack is to be eaten. This activity will make a great snack or a very special breakfast activity.

Spreading Butter & Pouring Syrup Over a Waffle

Materials Needed

- ❖ Waffle
- ❖ A Small Dish with an Individual Portion of Softened Butter
- ❖ A Syrup Dispenser
- ❖ An Individual Plate
- ❖ Blunt Knife and Child Size Fork
- ❖ Display Tray

Presentation and Activity:

Demonstrate for the child how to first spread the butter over the waffle. Next, show the child how to squeeze the syrup dispenser with his thumb in order to open the lid and allow the syrup to pour. Pick up the syrup dispenser and hold it over the waffle. Proceed to pour using two hands, as in the other pouring exercising, while continuing to press on the lever. Slowly pour the syrup over the waffle.

This application also includes cutting skills. Holding the fork in the nondominant hand, place it into the waffle to hold it secure. Use the knife in the dominant hand to make sawing motions and cut through the waffle.

Waffles can be prepared from scratch or purchased as frozen and simply placed in a toaster or warmed in a microwave for the activity. As always, take care that the food is not too hot for a small child.

As you can tell, what seems like a simple activity actually involves many fine motor skills for a small child. Take the time to demonstrate each step and assist the child in the early stages as he discovers how to utilize all of these skills. The fun reward at the end is enjoying the delicious waffle that took effort and concentration to prepare. This activity is set up as an activity that is prepared and eaten in the same area; therefore the utensils are included in the activity.

Packaging Eggs

Materials Needed

- ❖ A Basket Lined with a Kitchen Towel
- ❖ One Dozen Fresh Eggs (Not Cooked)
- ❖ An Egg Carton
- ❖ Kitchen Towel or Mat

Presentation and Activity:

Demonstrate for the children how to carefully handle the eggs. Carefully place up one egg and place it in an indention in the carton. Repeat with all 12 eggs until the carton is filled. Then demonstrate how to close and latch the egg carton.

After completing this part of the activity, demonstrate for the child how to open the carton. Next, carefully pick up each egg and gently set it back inside the basket. The children can repeat the activity as much as they would like.

This activity requires fine motor skills along with both care and careful concentration. It can be expected that mistakes will be made and eggs will be broken. This is considered a logical consequence. From the experience the child will learn greater care and concentration in an effort to not break the eggs.

This is a wonderful and traditional Montessori activity with real world applications and consequences. Knowing some eggs will likely be broken, take additional steps in preparation for this activity. Place the activity in an area which can be easily cleaned. This includes both the work surface and the floor. Placing the activity on a washable mat or towel helps make clean up of any mistakes easier. In addition, have more eggs and towels available in case of breakages.

Cracking Eggs

Materials Needed

- ❖ A Bowl with Fresh Eggs
- ❖ A Smaller Bowl
- ❖ A Display Tray

Presentation and Activity:

Demonstrate how to carefully pick up one egg and tap it against the table. (For small children cracking the egg against the table is easier than against the rim of the bowl.) Show the children how to get the appropriate amount of cracking on the outside of the shell so that it will break gently. Demonstrate how to use your thumbs to push in gently on the crack and open the egg. Gently drop the egg into the bowl.

For a small child, cracking an egg can be very challenging. It takes great concentration and practice to do it well. Expect eggs to be full of shells or dropped outside of the bowl as the child works on the skill. Teach the child how to retrieve any small pieces of shell that fall into the bowl with the egg.

After completing this activity, it is a great time to make scrambled eggs or enjoy a cooking project which uses eggs such as baking a cake or cookies. Activities such as this have even greater authenticity and interest when they are combined with a project that uses the ingredients.

Peeling Hard Boiled Eggs

Materials Needed

- ❖ Hard Boiled Eggs (Cooled)
- ❖ A Small Bowl Filled with Water
- ❖ A Small Bowl for Egg Shells
- ❖ A Kitchen Towel
- ❖ A Display Tray

Presentation and Activity:

Begin the presentation by gently tapping the egg on the table. Tap the egg until it is well cracked on all sides. Next begin to gently peel back the egg shell. Gently peel the egg shell off. The water can be used to help remove small pieces of shell that stick to your fingers and the towel should be used to dry your fingers after using the water. (Note that eggs that have been stored in the refrigerator for a week or more, but are still within the packaging use by date, are best for peeling. Very fresh eggs do not peel easily and will make the activity difficult.)

After completing this activity, the child can proceed to a snack of eating the boiled egg. This snack could be combined with the next activity which involves slicing the egg. Other suggestions for using the eggs that are peeled include making egg salad or chopping the boiled egg with a blunt knife and seasoning it with a little salt.

Slicing Hard Boiled Eggs

Materials Needed

- ❖ Peeled Hard Boiled Eggs
- ❖ Egg Slicer
- ❖ A Small Serving Plate
- ❖ A Display Tray

Presentation and Activity:

Lay the egg into the slicer so that it fits correctly. Slowly pull the slicer down over the hard boiled eggs to slice. Next, while the slicer is still in the lowered position, remove the perfectly sliced egg as a whole unit and place it onto the serving dish. The result is a very pretty presentation of the boiled egg.

After the child completes the activity, he can take the egg to his place at the table, season it with a little bit of salt, and enjoy it.

This is a simple activity which can be easily completed by even very young children. The appearance of the perfectly sliced egg creates a great sense of accomplishment with minimal effort.

Using Tongs to Grasp Pickles

Materials Needed

- ❖ Jar of Pickles
- ❖ Small Tongs
- ❖ A Small Serving Plate
- ❖ A Display Tray

Presentation and Activity:

Take the lid off of the pickle jar and set it on the tray. Pick up the tongs and put them into the pickle jar. Pinch the tongs together to grab a pickle and pull it out. Lay the pickle on the plate. Place the pickle on the serving dish.

A small jar of pickles works best to more easily access the pickles. If you are preparing the activity for a group of children and need a larger jar (which will be much less expensive than multiple small jars of pickles), then pay attention to the level of the liquid inside the jar. As some of the pickles are removed, simply pour off some of the liquid to make it easier for children to access the pickles.

Sausages and Dip

Materials Needed

- ❖ Cocktail Sausages in a Small Bowl (Cooked, Then Cooled to Room Temperature)
- ❖ Squeeze Bottles of Ketchup and/or Mayonnaise
- ❖ Small Condiment Cups (1 or 2 Depending on the Number of Condiments)
- ❖ A Display Tray

Presentation and Activity:

Demonstrate for the child how to turn the bottle upside down and squeeze the condiments into the condiment cups. Show the child exactly how much of the condiment is appropriate to put into the cup. Pick up a small cocktail sausage and dip it into the condiment of choice and enjoy a snack.

If using the activity in a group setting. The set up could be set up as a buffet style activity to allow children to squeeze the condiments onto their individual plates (rather than into condiment cups), and serve themselves the cocktail sausages using small tongs. This would significantly reduce the number of dishes that are needed.

English Muffin Cheese Pizza

Materials Needed

- ❖ English Muffin Half
- ❖ Condiment Cup with Spaghetti Sauce
- ❖ Condiment Cup with Grated Mozzarella Cheese
- ❖ Small Spoon
- ❖ A Display Tray

Presentation and Activity:

Pick up the spoon and dip it into the spaghetti sauce. Then spread the spaghetti sauce over the English muffin. Next, pick up the condiment cup with cheese and sprinkle the cheese out of the condiment cup and over the English muffin. The snack is then ready to be enjoyed.

This can be set up as a single serving plate, as shown in the example, or it can be adapted and set up as a work station where each child will make his own English muffin pizza and then move it to an individual plate.

This is a very easy activity which is fun for even the youngest children. It can also be combined with grating cheese for a Practical Life activity that utilizes multiple processes.

Preparing a Bowl of Cereal

Materials Needed

- ❖ Cereal Bowl
- ❖ Pitcher filled with Milk
- ❖ Cereal (Preferably Unsweetened and Wholesome With Natural Color)
- ❖ Honey (or Other Natural Sweetener if Desired)
- ❖ Small Spoon
- ❖ A Display Tray

Presentation and Activity:

Pick up the box and tilt it toward the bowl. Carefully pour the cereal into the bowl using two hands. Show the child how one hand goes on the top and the other goes on the bottom of the box to control the pouring of the cereal. Slowly pour cereal into the bowl demonstrating how much to pour in and how to control the pouring process. Next, pick up the pitcher and proceed to demonstrate how to carefully pour the milk using two hands just as in all of the pouring exercises in Chapter 4. If desired, show the child how to drizzle the natural sweetener over the cereal.

This activity requires concentration and more refined fine motor skills. It is best incorporated into the program for children who have mastered the basic pouring exercises in early chapters.

Slicing a Banana

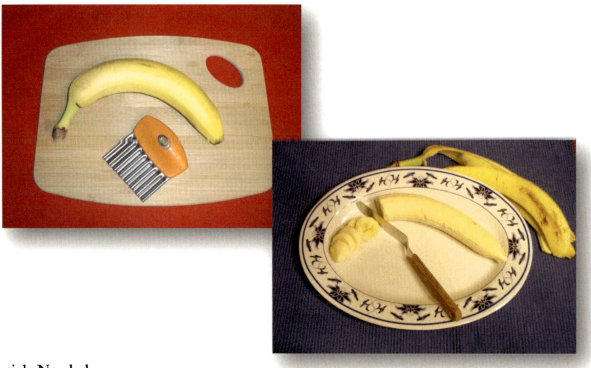

Materials Needed

- ❖ Banana
- ❖ Blunt Knife (or Other Safe Utensil for Cutting)
- ❖ A Display Tray

Presentation and Activity:

Snap the top of the banana stem by pulling it backwards. This is the most difficult part of the activity for children. Very young children may need this part completed before they begin the activity. Next, show the child how to peel the banana demonstrating each step in peeling and completing the demonstration by completely removing the banana peel. Show the child how to slice the banana into nice even slices.

This activity can include different utensils to create various slicing effects. A blunt knife as described is the first one. The example photos show variations including using a wavy slider in the first picture and using an icing spreader in the second example. The example photos also include variations in the display tray. A natural cutting board is a fun way to increase the authenticity of the Practical Life exercise and using attractive plates will make the activity more visually appealing.

This is an excellent activity, using real food, for very young children to practice. Bananas are easy to peel and slice and it makes a very enjoyable Practical Life exercise.

Picking Grapes off of the Stem

Caution: This is a simple activity which can easily be done by small children; however, use caution in choosing this activity for very small children because grapes do pose a choking hazard. For this reason, it is an appropriate activity only for children who are over two and are not prone to choking.

Materials Needed

- Small Bunch of Grapes
- Small Bowl
- Display Plate

Presentation and Activity:

Hold the bunch of grapes in the nondominant hand and pull a grape from the bunch using the dominant hand. Set the grape into the small bowl. Repeat the activity picking each individual grape from the bunch.

Scooping Melon Balls

Materials Needed

- One Cantaloupe Half (Seeds Removed)
- A Small Bowl
- Melon Ball Tool
- Work Tray

Presentation and Activity:

Pick up the melon ball tool. Push one side of the scoop into the fruit, push down and back up in a scooping motion to create a melon ball. Transfer the melon ball to the bowl and drop it in using the tool. Other seedless melons such as honey dew and seedless watermelons can be used in the process. Choose what is in season and what the children enjoy the most. It makes a healthy and delicious snack.

This is a very simple activity and is appropriate even for very young children.

Skewering Fruit & Cheese

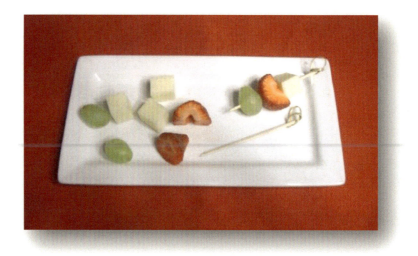

Caution: Skewers do contain sharp points which make the activity easy; however, it requires close supervision both while children complete the activity and if they are eating the fruit and cheese to ensure that they are not poked by the sharp end of the skewer. It is not recommended for very young children.

Materials Needed

- ❖ Small Slices of Fruit and Cheese
- ❖ Wooden Picks or Small Skewers
- ❖ Display Tray

Presentation and Activity:

Take a skewer in the nondominant hand. Then pick up a piece of fruit with the dominant hand. Skewer the fruit onto the wooden pick and push it down to the end. Then pick up another piece of cheese or fruit and continue to skewer each piece until the pick is full. Repeat the process with a second skewer. This is a wonderful activity to enjoy both the process of the work and the delicious snack.

Preparing Fruit Salad

Caution: Take care that the fruit choices are appropriate for the age children. Small fruits such as grapes can pose a choking risk to very small children.

Materials Needed

- A Variety of Fresh Fruit
- A Serving Bowl
- A Display Tray

Presentation and Activity:

This activity can encompass many different skills and may be designed to be complex or simplistic depending on which fruits you want to include and how much preparation is needed for those types of fruits. Determine what you would like for the activity to encompass and the appropriate fruits for completing the lesson. Fruits that are easy to prepare are recommended for the first time the activity is completed and then adding additional fruits which require more skill to prepare can be added when the activity is repeated at later times.

Depending on the fruits chosen and the ages of the children; activities can include peeling oranges, peeling and slicing bananas, picking grapes, hulling strawberries, and other such tasks.

Extension

The fruit salad activity can be set up as an individual serving rather than a large bowl. In this case, the fruit provided would be a small amount and a small individual size bowl would be utilized. Once complete, the child could eat her own fruit salad. This activity is probably best for completing with only one or a small number of children. The large fruit salad works best in a group setting.

This extension provides a very small serving for one individual child. It also extends the fruit salad to include whipped topping that is stirred into the fruit for a delicious fruit salad.

Slicing a Cucumber

Materials Needed

- ❖ A Cucumber or Zucchini
- ❖ A Wavy Cutter or Other Safe Cutting Tool
- ❖ A Cutting Board or other Display Tray

Presentation and Activity:

Demonstrate for the child how to hold the cucumber still with her nondominant hand and use the wavy slicer to press down on the cucumber with her dominant hand.

This activity is relatively simple for children who have mastered the more basic slicing using soft foods such as bananas. The wavy slicer provides a safe way to cut by using pressure pushing down which works better and is safer than a knife.

Mixing Dip

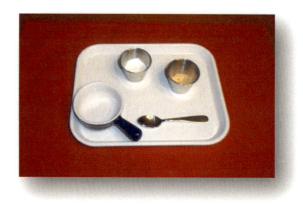

Materials Needed:

- ❖ One Condiment Cup with Sour Cream
- ❖ A Second Condiment Cup with Dry Ranch Dip Mix
- ❖ A Mixing Bowl
- ❖ A Small Spoon
- ❖ A Display Tray

Presentation and Activity:

Spoon the sour cream into the mixing bowl. Next, pick up the cup with ranch dip mix and pour it into the bowl. Pick up the spoon and stir the sour cream and dip mix. This is a great activity to combine with slicing the cucumber. Together they make a delicious and healthy snack.

Snapping Green Beans

Materials Needed

- ❖ Fresh (Raw) Green Beans
- ❖ Two Straw Baskets
- ❖ A Display Tray

Presentation and Activity:

Pick up a green bean. Hold it in the nondominant hand and using the dominant hand and "snap" off the tip end of the green bean. Then turn it over and snap off the other end. Let the ends fall back into the basket and put the freshly snapped green beans in the second basket. Repeat the activity. (You could add a third basket for the snapped ends if desired). After children complete the activity, you may want to cook the fresh green beans and enjoy them with lunch.

Because there is nothing particularly messy or that requires additional supervision, this activity could be used as a shelf activity if desired.

Extensions

This activity can be extended to include using a blunt knife and a cutting board. Place one green bean on the cutting board and cut off the ends. If desired, the activity can be further extended by adding the process of cutting the green beans into small pieces with the blunt knife.

Washing Root Vegetables

Materials Needed

- One or More Root Vegetables
- A Bowl of Water
- Child Size Vegetable Scrubber

Presentation and Activity:

Pick up a vegetable and place it in the water. Pick up the scrubber by the handle and use the brush end to clean the dirt off of the vegetable. Scrub it until it is clean and then continue with the other vegetables. You can add a kitchen towel to the activity if desired to dry the vegetables after scrubbing them.

This activity can be used repeatedly on the same few vegetables as a shelf activity or you can have numerous vegetables cleaned and then proceed to cook them. Scrubbing vegetables is a good activity for all ages. For older children, it could be combined with the peeling activity which follows and the vegetables could be used in a soup. Keep in mind peeling potatoes is more difficult for children than carrots and should only be included after peeling carrots has been mastered. This would be good for children who are a little older and have gained greater fine motor skills.

Peeling Carrots

Caution: This activity requires careful supervision and should not be utilized as a shelf activity due to the possibility of cuts from the blade of the peeler

Materials Needed

- Carrot
- Peeler
- Display Plate

Presentation and Activity:

Hold how to hold the carrot up right from the stem using the dominant hand. Next, hold the peeler with the dominant hand. Place peeler with the blade side against the step side of the carrot and pull down slowly to demonstrate how to peel the carrot. Allow the child to practice this skill.

This activity can be used to simply peel the carrot or the child can continue to peel until the carrot is very small creating many ribbons of carrot peelings. If the activity is used for an exercise then continuing to peel is recommended. If you are going to extend the activity and actually eat the carrot either raw or cooked, then be sure to discard the outer peel before proceeding to continue to make ribbons.

Grating a Carrot

Caution: Supervise the activity carefully and discard the base of the carrot well before it is close to the grater to avoid cutting the child's fingers on the grater.

Materials Needed

- ❖ Peeled Carrot
- ❖ Grater
- ❖ Display Plate

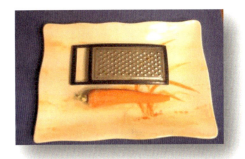

Presentation and Activity:

Hold the grater upright with the dominant hand. Next, hold the peeled carrot in the dominant hand and slowly push down to grate the carrot. This activity can be used as an extension of peeling a carrot. First complete the peeling a carrot activity then move on to grating it.

Preparing Carrot Salad

Materials Needed

- ❖ Grated Carrot in a Small Bowl
- ❖ Raisins in a Small Bowl
- ❖ Sweetened Condensed Milk in a Condiment Cup or Small Bowl
- ❖ Small Size Spoon
- ❖ Child Size Bowl for Mixing and Eating
- ❖ Display Tray

Presentation and Activity:

Take the grated carrot and spoon it into the larger bowl. Pick up the raisins and spoon them into the bowl. Then take the sweetened condensed milk and spoon it into the bowl. Proceed to gently mix the carrot salad. After the child has completed the process, he can enjoy the healthy snack.

This is a very simple activity which is appropriate for almost all children. As with other projects, when using this in a group, it can be set up differently to allow for a buffet or family style set up where each child can scoop from a serving bowl rather than have an individual set up.

Peeling an Orange

Materials Needed

- ❖ Small Orange (Preferably Clementine) on a Plate
- ❖ Bowl
- ❖ Display Tray

Presentation and Activity:

Make an initial tear in the orange. Then place your thumb in that tear and use your thumb and fingers to remove pieces of the orange peel. Place the peeling pieces into the bowl. Once the orange is completely peeled, push your thumb into the middle of the orange and separate the orange segments using your thumb and fingers.

This exercise is very good for fine motor skills with real authenticity. It can be challenging at first for young children but at it is also enjoyable and valuable. The child can enjoy the healthy snack after completing the process. Clementine's (or mandarin oranges) work best because they are both small and easy to peel. Very small children may need help with the first step of creating the initial tear into the orange peel; however, this activity is well suited for most children.

Preparing Fun Shaped Sandwiches

Materials Needed

- ❖ Prepared Sandwich
- ❖ Selected Cookie or Sandwich Cutters
- ❖ Individual Plates
- ❖ Display Tray

Presentation and Activity:

Press the sandwich cutter into the sandwich to create the shape. Tear the excess bread away from the cookie cutter. It reveals a fun shape for the sandwich.

Extension 1

A fun extension for this activity is the use of a small sandwich cutter. This utilizes a different skill as children press down on the cutter and then pull it out. The top of the tool is then pressed to release the sandwich cut out. It provides a fun way to make and eat small sandwiches.

More Extensions

These activities can be combined with actually preparing the sandwich if a more comprehensive activity is desired.

7
Cleaning and Organizing

Sorting Flatware

Caution: Both sorting flatware and setting the table are simple activities. However, take care to only include blunt knives to ensure safety. Supervise the activities carefully as both blunt knives and even forks can create hazards if misused in a group environment.

Materials Needed

- ❖ A Basket Lined with a Towel
- ❖ Flatware
- ❖ Flatware Sorter Tray
- ❖ Work Mat

Presentation and Activity:

Begin with the flatware in the basket. Pick up a piece of flatware and place it in the correct location in the sorting tray. Pick up another piece of flatware and continue the process until all of the flatware is correctly placed in the sorting tray. Remove all of the pieces and place them back into the basket.

Setting the Table

Materials Needed

- ❖ A Basket Lined with a Towel
- ❖ Flatware
- ❖ Plate
- ❖ Drinking Cup
- ❖ Placemat

Presentation and Activity:

Lay the placemat flat on a table. Next, place the plate in the center of the placemat. Continue to place each of the items in their correct place as shown in the example. This would be a good activity to incorporate into a mealtime. After completing the placement, the child can eat at her place setting.

Washing Dishes

Caution: Even with only a small amount of water, this activity requires an adult carefully supervising to ensure the activity is safe for small children.

Materials Needed

- ❖ A Large Bucket or Pot filled with Water
- ❖ Dish Soap if Desired for Bubbles
- ❖ Various Small Bowls or Other Dishes
- ❖ One or More Types of Dish Scrubbers
- ❖ Kitchen Towel
- ❖ An Absorbent Work Mat

Presentation and Activity:

Pick up a dish and place it into the wash bucket. Scrub the dish with one of the scrubbers. After washing the dish, take the towel and dry it.

Extensions:

This activity can also be extended by utilizing a separate tub for rinsing and adding a dish drying rack if desired.

Organizing Canned Goods

Materials Needed

- ❖ Canned Goods (3 of Each Item)
- ❖ Graduated Cabinet Organizer

Presentation and Activity:

Pick up a can and place it on the storage rack. Next, pick up another can and repeat the procedure. Place cans which have the same contents on the same row. Continue until all cans are organized into rows based on the contents.

This can also be done as an activity by putting the items directly into your kitchen shelf if you have a low cabinet where canned goods can be stored, which is easily accessible to children.

Washing Clothes

Caution: Use only non-toxic child safe soap for suds. The activity can be completed using only water if desired. Even with only a small amount of water, this activity requires an adult carefully supervising to ensure the activity is safe for small children.

Materials Needed

- A Large Bucket or Pot filled with Soapy Water
- A Straw Basket with Child Size Clothes
- Scrub Board
- Absorbent Mat

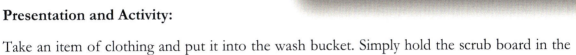

Presentation and Activity:

Take an item of clothing and put it into the wash bucket. Simply hold the scrub board in the water and rub the clothes up and down on the ridges or the board.

This is a fun old fashioned and timeless Practical Life activity that children enjoy.

Extensions:

An additional bucket of clean water can be added for rinsing if desired. This can also be combined with the activity of hanging clothes on a line or rack to dry.

Hanging Clothes

Materials Needed

- A Small Laundry Basket
- Various Child Size Clothes
- Child Size Hangers (Not Wire)
- Work Mat

Presentation and Activity:

Pick up a shirt and a hanger. Hold the shirt right side up. Slide the hanger through the opening at the base of the shirt. Push the hanger up through the neck hole of the shirt. Push the sides of the hanger into the sleeves of the shirt. Lay the hung items down on the mat or, if you have room, you can provide something to hang them on. Continue the hanging process with pants, sweaters, and other clothing items. Be sure the present how to hang each item that requires a different skill.

Folding Wash Cloths

Materials Needed

- A Small Laundry Basket
- Wash Cloths
- Work Mat

Presentation and Activity:

Pick up a wash cloth. Fold it over in half. Smooth the edges so that it lies flat. Then fold it over in the other direction creating a square. Smooth it flat again and lay it on the mat. Continue the activity. Stack the folded wash cloths neatly. This is a good activity to use as a shelf activity. It is also great to utilize with actual laundry either at home or in a child care center. Demonstrate how to fold the wash cloths and stack them on top of each other.

This is a fun and simple Practical Life activity for even the youngest children. Both the folding and rolling socks activities make great shelf materials that can be left out all of the time. This is also a good skill to practice at home while helping with the laundry.

Extension:

You can also put up wash cloths by rolling them or folding them over into rectangles instead of squares to vary the activity.

Matching and Rolling Socks

Materials Needed

- A Small Laundry Basket
- Multiple Pairs of Socks
- Work Mat

Presentation and Activity:

Choose a sock. Find a sock that matches it. Fold the top of one sock over the other so that they remain rolled together. Repeat the process.

Clipping Clothes Pins

Caution: This activity can be difficult for very small children. Make sure the child has the strength to squeeze the clothes pins open with his dominant hand before using either of the activities involving clothes pins. If the child can't complete the activity using only one hand, then he may try to use both hands which can lead to pinching the fingers.

Materials Needed

- A Small Bucket or Basket
- Clothes Pins
- Work Mat

Presentation and Activity:

Pick up a clothes pin. Squeeze the handle portion and clip the other side onto the edges of the bucket. Repeat the activity.

Hanging Small Towels

Materials Needed

- Small Hanging Rack
- Wash Cloths in a Straw Basket
- Clothes Pins
- Work Mat

Presentation and Activity:

Take a towel and place it over a wire on the hanging rack. Pick up a clothes pin and squeeze the handles to open them and then attach them to the wire securing the cloth.

This is a good activity to use after the basic clothes pin activity has been mastered. It extends the basic skill. It allows for further mastery and concentration by actually clipping objects.

The rack used in the photo is an item which is used to create an additional level inside a kitchen cabinet (found in the kitchen accessory section of a discount store). It is small and the wash cloths were cut into quarters to fit. As always when creating your own materials use what is available and inexpensive and create ways to make these items work.

Dusting

Materials Needed

- ❖ Selected Dusting Materials
- ❖ Basket

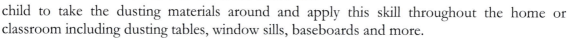

The dusting materials selected can vary. The items in the example include a microfiber duster with handle, a microfiber cloth towel duster, and a feather duster. You can include one item or several.

Presentation and Activity:

Demonstrate how to use each of the dusting materials which are available to the child. Allow the child to take the dusting materials around and apply this skill throughout the home or classroom including dusting tables, window sills, baseboards and more.

Children really enjoy doing basic cleaning activities that they see their parents doing. Dusting is usually a favorite activity.

Sweeping

Materials Needed

- ❖ Small Hand Sweeper and Dust Pan
- ❖ Small Grains to Sweep
- ❖ Display Tray

Presentation and Activity:

Sprinkle the grains onto the display tray and then demonstrate how to sweep the grains into the dust pan. Use the dominant hand to hold the sweeper and the other hand to hold the dust pan against the tray. Use a gentle sweeping motion to push the grains into the dust pan with the sweeper. After sweeping all of the grains into the dust pan, pour the materials back into the basket and the activity is ready to be repeated.

.

Cleaning Lint

Materials Needed

- ❖ Towels or Other Fabric – Preferably Dark Colors that Show Lint
- ❖ Small Travel Size Lint Roller
- ❖ Basket

Presentation and Activity:

Unroll the towels and roll the sticky tape of the roller over the towels to collect lint. After the roller is covered with lint, show the child how to remove one layer of sticky tape from the roller. Repeat the activity as desired.

The activity can include cleaning lint on other surfaces such as curtains and upholstered chairs. Another suggestion is that the dark towels can be washed with light towels to create more lint to clean if desired.

Cleaning Windows

Materials Needed

- ❖ Spray Bottle Filled with Water and a Splash of Vinegar
- ❖ Small Soft Towels
- ❖ Basket

Presentation and Activity:

Hold the bottle and point the spray nozzle at a window. Squeeze the handle once or twice to disperse vinegar on the window. Use the towels to wipe the window clean. Repeat as desired.

Notes: Vinegar makes a safe non-toxic cleaner for children. Chemical based cleaners should not be used in activities for children. Older Montessori activities will include some cleaners which are questionable for children. These should always be replaced with something that will work but is safe for children.

Extension:

If desired, the bottle can be filled with water to clean other surfaces, such as tables, floors, and window sills.

Opening and Closing

Caution: If small pieces are included, such as in the example here, the activity should not be provided to children under the age of three due to posing a choking hazard. The activity is appropriate for very young children; however, all items including lids, must meet the criteria for being large enough to not pose a choking hazard.

Materials Needed

- ❖ Various Containers Which Require Different Skills to Open and Close.
- ❖ Basket

Presentation and Activity:

This activity can be presented in a Montessori format by showing the child how each container can be opened and closed. It can also be utilized as an exploratory activity. In using this method, the child can work at exploring the concept of exactly what skills are needed to open and close each container.

Extension:

Once the basic activity is mastered, you may want to add "surprises" into the containers. Small plastic toys or other items will add additional interest to the activity as there is something new to explore when containers are opened.

8
Care of Self and Others

Combing and Brushing Hair

Caution: The activities on this page are for an individual child. If done in a preschool setting, each child would require his own set of materials. Therefore, this is not appropriate for a shelf activity.

Materials Needed

- ❖ Comb, Brush, or Both
- ❖ Mirror (Handheld or on a Wall)
- ❖ Display Tray

Presentation and Activity:

Demonstrate for the child how to comb or brush her hair. This demonstration would be done on the child's own hair and each child must have an individual comb or brush if utilizing this activity in a center. Show her how to use the mirror to see how her hair looks and if she needs to work more on the brushing or the work is complete.

Brushing Teeth

Materials Needed

- ❖ Child Size Toothbrush
- ❖ Travel Size Toothpaste
- ❖ Cup for Rinsing
- ❖ Mirror (Hand Held or Wall Mounted)
- ❖ A Sink
- ❖ A Stool (If Needed)
- ❖ Display Tray

Presentation and Activity:

Begin the demonstration by showing the child how to rinse the toothbrush with water. Next, show her how to take the lid off of the toothpaste. Squeeze a small amount of toothpaste onto the brush. Then, demonstrate for the child how to correctly brush her teeth. Explain the procedures for brushing all of her teeth until they are clean, spitting out the toothpaste, and rinsing her mouth with water. After she has completed brushing, demonstrate how to rinse the toothbrush off and store it for the next use.

Packing a Lunch Box

Materials Needed

- ❖ Selected Food and a Drinks for Lunch
- ❖ Ice Pack
- ❖ Napkin (Paper or Cloth)
- ❖ Lunch Kit or Paper Bag

Presentation and Activity:

Demonstrate how to pack a lunch correctly including concepts such as placing the ice pack next to the items which should be kept cold; packing the heavier things on the bottom; and the more fragile items on the top. This can be used as a shelf activity including items which are not perishable and can sit on the shelf for a few days (and be updated as needed). It can also be used as a more comprehensive activity including having the child pack his lunch for the day and eating it at lunch time. It can be an even more comprehensive activity when combined with the following extensions.

Extensions:

You can extend the activity further by having children make their own sandwich, freeze their own ice packs, choosing appropriate healthy lunch supplies, and even going grocery shopping to select food for their lunches. This is a great time to incorporate the concepts of healthy eating and good choices while selecting food. Another extension would include learning to pack a "no waste lunch" where all of the packaging is prepared in re-usable containers and the napkin is cloth so that there is no trash.

Packing a Picnic Basket

Materials Needed

- ❖ Selected Food and Drinks for Two or More People
- ❖ Napkin (Paper or Cloth)
- ❖ Picnic Basket
- ❖ Picnic Blanket or Towel

Presentation and Activity:

This activity is similar to packing a lunch box. The difference is this activity is designed to be taken outdoors and eaten. It is prepared in a traditional picnic basket format for authenticity and old fashioned fun. Demonstrate how to properly prepare a lunch and then pack the food into the basket. The heavy items should be placed at the bottom of the basket and the lighter or more fragile items should be placed on the top. Then take the picnic basket outside and enjoy!

Extension:

The picnic can be prepared in a cooler with ice and taken to a selected location. This is particularly good for family outings and field trips in child care centers. The food and event is more fun if the children are allowed to participate in the process of selecting, preparing, and packaging the food for the event.

Packing an Overnight Bag

Materials Needed

- ❖ Child's Clothes, Underwear, Socks, and Shoes
- ❖ Toothpaste and Toothbrush
- ❖ Mirror and Comb
- ❖ Pajamas
- ❖ Accessories such as a Hat and Stuffed Toy
- ❖ Small Overnight Bag
- ❖ Basket to Hold Supplies (If Desired for Shelf Activity)

Presentation and Activity:

Unzip the bag and open it. Next, fold the clothes and place them carefully into the overnight bag. Add the personal items and accessories. Finally, close the bag. The child can complete the activity by unpacking the bag and placing the materials back into the basket so that the activity is ready to be repeated.

This can easily be set up as a shelf activity. Simply set the basket of materials on a shelf and set the overnight case beside the shelf. During the demonstration, explain how the pieces work together and that it is one activity.

Extensions:

In a preschool this is best utilized as a shelf activity. For your child at home, this is an excellent learning activity to combine with an overnight stay at a friend's house or going to visit a grandparent. Extend the activity by allowing the child to think about what needs to go into an overnight back, making selections on the clothes he would like to wear, and packing these things into the bag. After the trip, he should unpack the bag and place everything where it belongs back at home.

Dressing Skills

In Montessori programs, the dressing frames are a basic learning material. These boards isolate each activity of dressing into a single activity. You can do the same thing in your home or classroom without having to purchase a set of expensive Montessori dressing frames. Most of the items for dressing skills can be found in your closets at home.

Buttoning

Materials Needed

- ❖ Two or More Large Pieces of Felt
- ❖ Large Buttons
- ❖ Scissors
- ❖ Needle and Thread
- ❖ Display Basket

For this activity, you will create the activity as follows:

Sew large size buttons onto one whole piece of felt. Cut the other felt pieces into squares. Cut a slit in the felt squares. The slit should be large enough to easily go over the large buttons. You are done!

Presentation and Activity:

Pick up a felt square. Place it over a button. Push the button through the hole on the felt square. Repeat with the remaining buttons. Once complete, unbutton the buttons by stretching the hole back over the button and pulling the felt square off. Put the square back into the basket.

Alternate Buttoning Material: If you prefer, you can select a shirt out of a closet which has buttons and use that for the buttoning activity. Note that standard clothing will likely have smaller buttons which may be more difficult for very young children.

Tying and Lacing

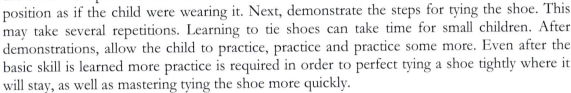

Materials Needed

- ❖ One Child's Shoe with Laces
- ❖ Display Basket

Presentation and Activity:

Face the shoe with the toe pointing away from the child. This puts the shoe in the exact same position as if the child were wearing it. Next, demonstrate the steps for tying the shoe. This may take several repetitions. Learning to tie shoes can take time for small children. After demonstrations, allow the child to practice, practice and practice some more. Even after the basic skill is learned more practice is required in order to perfect tying a shoe tightly where it will stay, as well as mastering tying the shoe more quickly.

Extension: After the child has mastered tying the shoe, you may demonstrate how to lace the shoe. Including a basket with a shoe that requires Velcro style fastener would also be a nice addition to your dressing skills materials.

Snapping and Zipping

Materials Needed

- ❖ One Pair of Child's Jeans or Shorts with a Snap and Zipper
- ❖ Display Basket

Presentation and Activity:

For the snap, line up the upper and lower portions of the snap. Push the two together to snap it closed. When complete, unsnap the snap by grasping both the top and bottom material around the snap and pulling.

For the zipper, grasp the tab on the zipper and pull it up. In order to unzip the jeans, grasp the zipper tab and pull down.

The main difference in using a pair of jeans or shorts for this activity would be that it does not "isolate" the activity. In other words the activity includes both snapping and zipping in one activity where as Montessori dressing boards would only have one learning objective such as a set of snaps on one board and a zipper on a separate board.

Dressing a Baby

The Montessori Method does not embrace playing with traditional toys such as dolls; however, the addition of a doll, for practicing dressing and bathing skills, is very enjoyable for children.

Materials Needed

- ❖ Doll
- ❖ Doll Clothing
- ❖ Doll Blanket (Optional)
- ❖ Basket

Presentation and Activity:

For very young children, a demonstration is appropriate to show how to get the clothes on and off. This requires skills that are still developing in young children and may be challenging. For older children, a demonstration may not be necessary as they can work on completing the process without instruction. This makes a good shelf activity.

Bathing a Baby

Caution: Even with only a small amount of water, this activity requires an adult carefully supervising to ensure the activity is safe for small children.

Materials Needed

- ❖ Plastic Doll (Appropriate for Water)
- ❖ Small Towel
- ❖ Small Wash Cloth
- ❖ Doll Bathtub or a Plastic Tub

Presentation and Activity:

Fill the bathtub with only a small amount of water. This will make it easier for children to work on the activity without spilling. Demonstrate how to wash the baby while keeping the water inside the tub.

Extensions:

For older children, a small amount of soap or bubble bath can be added to the water for bubbles in the tub. The same process could also be ued to wash plastic animals for a fun extension.

9
Art and Design

Scissor Skills

Materials Needed

- ❖ Scrapbook Patterned Paper or Other Selected Paper
- ❖ Child Scissors
- ❖ Envelope
- ❖ Work Tray

Presentation and Activity:

Hold the the scissors in the dominant hand with the thumb on the top. Next, hold the paper in the other hand. Make slow and precise cuts by fully opening and closing the scissors. This provides a straight cut in a line. Practice this skill by cutting out pictures from the patterned paper. The paper cuttings can be put into the envelope to keep.

Extension 1

The activity can be completed as shown above but instead of placing the paper cuttings in the envelope, incorporate gluing skills. This is another important skill. Be sure to demonstrate how much glue is appropriate and how to smear it over the back of the paper cutting so that it sticks to the paper.

Extension 2

Create new reasons to cut by providing children's wildlife magazines or age appropriate magazines that will have pictures the children will enjoy cutting out and keeping.

Each of the cutting skill activities is a good shelf activity for children who have demonstrated they can appropriately use scissors. For younger children who have not mastered scissors or may cut inappropriate things with those scissors, this should be a carefully supervised activity.

Sharpening Pencils

Notes: Supervise this activity carefully as pencils can be sharp and some children will even put their fingers into a pencil sharpener.

Materials Needed

- ❖ Hand Held Pencil Sharpener
- ❖ Pencils
- ❖ Two Cups to Hold the Pencils
- ❖ Work Tray

Presentation and Activity:

Set the display up with the pencils on the left. Hold the pencil in the dominant hand and hold the sharpener in the other hand. Slowly twist the pencil while holding the sharpener still. Take it out and demonstrate how to check if the pencil is sharp. Continue to sharpen the pencil until it is sharp. Set the sharpened pencil down in the second cup. Repeat the process with another pencil. After sharpening several pencils, demonstrate how to take the sharpener to a trash can, open the sharpener and empty the shavings into the trash can. Put the sharpener back together; return to the activity, and the child can repeat the activity or place it back on the shelf. If desired, a bowl can be added to the display so that the sharpener can be emptied at the child's workspace.

Writing a Note

Materials Needed

- ❖ Writing Paper
- ❖ Pencil
- ❖ Eraser
- ❖ Envelope
- ❖ Work Tray

Presentation and Activity:

Hold the pencil correctly in the dominant hand. (Always reinforce how to correctly hold a pencil.) Allow the child to write a note if she is able to write or draw a picture if that is what she would like to do. Show her how to correctly use the eraser by holding it in her dominant hand. Rub the eraser on the paper while holding the paper securely with the other hand. Brush off any eraser shavings and have her complete the work. Next, to complete the activity, demonstrate how to carefully fold the paper into thirds so that it fits into the envelope. Close the envelope to complete the activity.

Stringing

Materials Needed

- ❖ Cheerios or Other Circular Cereal
- ❖ Small Bowl for the Cereal
- ❖ Pipe Cleaners
- ❖ Work Tray

Presentation and Activity:

Begin by showing the child how to hold the pipe cleaner by the middle with his nondominant hand. Using the dominant hand, demonstrate how to string the cereal onto the pipe cleaners.

Extensions:

There are many ways to extend this activity. This can be extended into using colored cereal and creating patterns. The pipe cleaners can also be covered in the cereal, loop them around twice and connect the ends for a bracelet. Multiple pipe cleaners can be connected to make a longer creation or formed into different shapes. Additional extensions could include using beads instead of cereal.

Balancing Objects

Caution: This activity contains small parts and should not be used for children who may put the pieces in their mouths as this would pose a choking hazard.

Materials Needed

- ❖ Rocks
- ❖ Golf Tees
- ❖ Styrofoam Block
- ❖ Baskets to Hold the Materials

Presentation and Activity:

Insert the golf tees into the Styrofoam block. Next balance a rock on the top of each tee.

Extension 1

For rocks with a relatively flat surface, the child can work on balancing a second rock on top of the first one.

Extension 2

Use different materials to stack on top of the golf tees such as marbles, marshmallows, or other objects which will balance.

Additional extensions include creative layouts of the golf tees, and creating patterns of materials when using varied materials such as rocks.

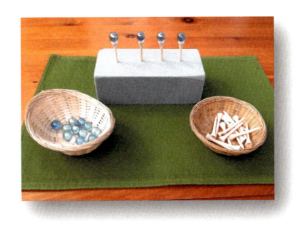

Weaving Ribbon

Materials Needed

- ❖ Long Strips of Ribbon
- ❖ Small Dish Shelf Insert
- ❖ Basket

Presentation and Activity:

Take a single ribbon from the basket and demonstrate how to weave the ribbon in and out of the wires. Then take another ribbon and start one wire further up so that it creates the alternating pattern creating the woven look.

Extensions:

There are numerous variations for ribbon weaving that can be created on a large scale such as in the example. A plastic laundry basket can make a good surface for weaving with very long ribbon strips. Look around for anything that would provide structure for weaving. This is a great activity for even very young children. The larger scale surfaces allow easier skill building for small fingers.

Paper Weaving

Materials Needed

- ❖ 1 Sheet of Construction Paper cut into Strips
- ❖ 1 Full Sheet of Another Color of Construction Paper
- ❖ Rules
- ❖ Scissors
- ❖ Work Tray

Presentation and Activity:

Take the large piece of paper and fold it in half. Mark straight lines across one side of the paper. Cut straight lines across the fold of the paper creating strips but without going to the edges of the paper so that the whole sheet remains intact. Next, take one strip of the construction paper and weave it in and out of the cut lines in the large sheet of paper. Take another strip of paper and weave it using the opposite sequence so that the weaving pattern appears as shown in the example.

For very young children, you may want to prepare the weaving board for them. Older children can make their own strips of paper.

Sewing on a Styrofoam Plate

Materials Needed

- ❖ Styrofoam Plate
- ❖ Child Scissors
- ❖ Large Plastic Embroidery Needle
- ❖ Yarn
- ❖ Work Tray

Presentation and Activity:

Cut a piece of yarn. Thread the needle with the yarn. Tie a knot at the end of the yarn. Take the threaded needle and place it against the back of the paper plate. Push it through to the front of the plate. Then push the needle back through the plate to the back. Continue to sew the plat in any design the child would like. After the sewing is complete, make sure to complete the project by pushing the needle to the back of the Styrofoam plate so that the loose end is on the back side. There is no need to tie it. This is a perfect first sewing project for children.

Extension:

The child can draw a pattern that she would like onto the plate and then work to sew the design onto the plate following the outline.

Sewing on Paper

Materials Needed

- ❖ Heavy Paper or Cardstock
- ❖ Hole Punch
- ❖ Child Scissors
- ❖ Large Plastic Embroidery Needle
- ❖ Yarn
- ❖ Basket

Presentation and Activity:

Punch holes around the outer edges of the paper.
Cut off the appropriate amount of yarn. Next, show the child how to thread the needle with the yarn and knot the end. (Small children may need help with this part.) Begin sewing in and out of the holes on the paper. After completing the work, the child will cut the yarn and knot the end of the yarn to secure the thread when sewn.

Small children will need additional help on some parts of the activities including additional help with preparation and finishing off the project. The completed project can be taken home.

Sewing a Button

Caution: The sewing projects which use sharp needles should be available to older children who have mastered the basic sewing processes using plastic needles and yarn.

Materials Needed

- Piece of Felt
- Large Button
- Heavy Embroidery Thread
- Large Embroidery Needle
- Child Scissors
- Tray

Presentation and Activity:

First show the child how to thread the needle. The large needle and embroidery thread will make this easier for young children. Place a knot in the end of the thread. This will also make it easier for young children to manage the sewing process. Next, hold the button on with the other hand and bring the needs up from under the felt with the dominant hand. Loop the thread into another hole in the button and pull it back to the underside. Repeat the process until the button is secure. Use the scissors to cut the extra thread and needle off.

Extensions:

For older children and children who have mastered sewing on the paper, sewing on pieces of felt is a good extension. This would include most of the same types of materials and methods that were used in the more basic sewing activities. The main difference is that it would utilize pieces of felt and a smaller sewing needle. A second extension would be using material secured through an embroidery hoop or a piece of cloth. The children would then simply sew on the cloth using regular sewing needles.

As children become proficient at this step additional extensions can be utilized, including smaller needles, regular sewing thread, multiple buttons, knotting thread, and sewing with a single strand of thread.

An art canvas can make a good base for sewing as well. And a final extension idea would be utilizing a large piece of cloth either loose or secured to a wooden structure for support. This large cloth can become a group sewing project. It can be left out as a classroom activity and used by all of the children in a classroom setting.

Scissor Skills

Materials Needed

- Paint Sample Cards
- Child Size Scissors
- Envelope
- Basket

Presentation and Activity:

Hold the card in their nondominant hand. First, hold the scissors up with the thumb on top and place them next to the white line between the colors on the left side of the paint sample card. Cut directly on the white line to separate one piece from the color card. After all of the colors are cut apart, then the pieces can be inserted into the envelope to keep.

Extensions:

The cut pieces can be used for sorting different colors, color identification, art projects with glue and even as a sensorial color grading activity where the pieces are reconstructed by the color shades from light to dark.

Stretching Bands

Caution: This activity contains small parts which may pose a choking hazard. See the extensions for adapting the activity for very young children.

Materials Needed

- Soft Hair Bands
- Narrow Paper Tube (From a Roll of Foil or Plastic Wrap) or a Dowel Rod
- Basket
- Work Tray

Presentation and Activity:

Select a band. Using the fingers of the dominant hand, stretch the band out and place it over the tube. Choose another band and repeat the process. After the bands are all on the tube, the child can take them off one by one and place them back in the basket

Extensions:

This activity can be extended to incorporate sensorial activities such as sorting by color and early math applications such as creating pattern with the colors. For very young children, this activity is a good development skill; however, until the fine motor skills are more defined, these children may benefit from adapting the project to include large bands and a tube with a large diameter to accommodate for the large bands. In addition, these larger materials will not pose the choking hazard inherent in using small pieces.

Threading Beads

Materials Needed

- ❖ Block of Floral Foam
- ❖ Chenille Stems
- ❖ Natural Colored Beads
- ❖ Basket
- ❖ Tray or Work Mat

Presentation and Activity:

Take a chenille stem and push it into the floral foam. Repeat the process with the remainder of the chenille stems. Pick up a bead and place the opening over the chenille stem. Push it down to the base of the stem. Choose another bead and continue the process. After the activity is complete, the child can then remove the beads and put them back into the basket. This continues the fine motor practice as well as completes the activity of cleaning up and preparing the materials to be placed back on the shelf to be used again.

Extensions:

The activity can be extended by having the child string the beads on the chenille stems without including the floral foam base. This is a more difficult task as the beads may slide off the other end if the fine motor skills are not carefully controlled.

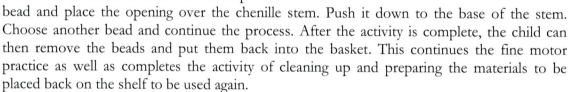

The process can be extended to include creating a circle. Twist the ends together and then secure them with tape or another bead where the wire meets. Be sure to completely cover the wire portion by wrapping it with the tape securely or making sure it is covered by the beads.

Stringing Beads for a Necklace

Materials Needed

- ❖ Cording
- ❖ Beads
- ❖ Tape (Optional)
- ❖ Scissors (Optional)
- ❖ Tray

Presentation and Activity:

Create a knot in the cord on one side. The knot should be large enough to hold the beads on the string while stringing them. If desired, the cord can be taped to the tray to secure it instead of a utilizing a large knot. Next, select a bead, and run the cord through the hole. Push the bead down to the base of the string. Continue to string beads until the necklace is complete. Once the necklace is compete tie the ends of the string together.

Depending on the age and ability of the child, the cording can be pre-cut to size or the cording can be included and the child can cut the string to the appropriate size.

Cornmeal Art

Materials Needed

- ❖ Cornmeal
- ❖ Tray

Presentation and Activity:

This is a very simple activity and suitable for children of all ages. Simply provide the cornmeal pressed into a tray or you can put it in a tub if you prefer. The child can create pictures with their fingers in the cornmeal. This creates an application of Practical Life, art, and sensory materials.

Extensions:

This activity can be completed with different materials; including salt, sand, grits, and other such materials. This is also a great way to extend Practical Life into other subject areas such as writing. The child can practice writing her letters or numbers in the cornmeal. This is perfect in the spirit on Montessori learning.

Additional extensions would be to provide other materials to create a variety of different patterns, experiences, and pictures in the cornmeal. Just look around at what is available. The items in the picture are examples of such materials. You can also add other material such as rocks, marbles, etc to create the feel of a zen garden. The children can create a beautiful piece of art while relaxing with the feel of the materials.

Making Colored Salt

Caution: This activity requires careful supervision to avoid children's fingers being cut with the grater. In addition, be sure to replace the chalk well before it is small enough to create a hazard of children accidently grating their fingers rather than the chalk.

Materials Needed

- ❖ Colored Chalk
- ❖ Grater
- ❖ Bowl of Table Salt
- ❖ Spoon
- ❖ Tray

Presentation and Activity:

Take a piece of colored chalk and grate it into a fine powder. Add the powdered chalk to the salt and stir with the spoon. It makes beautiful colored salt. The activity can be enjoyed as a Practical Life skill or you can extend it into an art projects such as those in the extensions.

Extensions:

The colored salt can be used in place of sand for sand art projects, glued on paper, and even sprinkled like glitter.

Creating Rubbings

Materials Needed

- ❖ Paper Squares
- ❖ Crayons
- ❖ Tray

Presentation and Activity:

Peel the paper wrapper off of the crayons. Next, take the paper and crayon around the home or school and look for interesting textures. These can be found anywhere. Floor tiles will show squares when rubbed, walls will show texture, and wood will show lines. There are even more textures if you can take the activity outdoors. Trees, concrete, bricks, and much more are all available outdoors.

After finding an interesting texture, place the paper against it. Lay the crayon on its side and "rub" it over the paper. The texture of the surface will show through. Use a different paper for each surface and then let the children enjoy comparing the rubbings. It is fun, creative, artistic, and creates a sensory learning experience.

Gift Wrapping With Bags

Materials Needed

- ❖ Small Gifts
- ❖ Small Gift Bags
- ❖ Ribbons or Bows
- ❖ Tissue Paper
- ❖ Tape (Optional)
- ❖ Tray

Presentation and Activity:

Place the gift item into the bag. Then take a piece of tissue paper and pinch it in the center and use your other hand to form the tissue into a cone shape. Next, push the middle "pinched" area into the center of the bag and let the rest of the tissue spread out. Add more tissue paper if desired. Take the ribbon and apply it to the bag with the adhesive attached to it or use tape. (Tape will need to be used if the activity is used in a center and utilized repeatedly.)

The gift is ready to give, or if you are using it as a shelf activity, remove the ribbons, take the tissue paper out, remove the gift, and its ready to use again.

Gift Wrapping Boxes

Materials Needed

- ❖ Small Box
- ❖ Small Roll of Gift Wrap (Cut From a Roll)
- ❖ Ribbons or Bows
- ❖ Tape
- ❖ Scissors
- ❖ Tray

Presentation and Activity:

Roll out the gift wrap. Center the small box on the roll. Cut off the extra paper. Fold the gift wrap around the box and tape it down. This will be the bottom. Turn the box over so that the tape is on the bottom. Next show the child how to create the corner folds and tape them down. Tape the ribbon or bow onto the top of the box and the project is complete.

This is best as a project activity since unwrapping the box will not lead to a nice result when another child attempts the project. The box could be wrapped as a single activity or it would be great when combined with a holiday, such as Mother's Day or Father's Day, when the child will be giving a gift he has made.

10
Construction

Hammering

Caution: Take care to protect your surfaces when doing hammering activities, particularly if the children are going to complete them on a table. Surfaces can be easily damaged when children are enjoying the hammering process.

Materials Needed

- ❖ Nails
- ❖ Floral Foam Block
- ❖ Child Size Wood Mallet
- ❖ Tray

Presentation and Activity:

Pick up a nail and hold it on top of the floral foam board with the nondominant hand. Take the mallet in the dominant hand and use it to gently hammer the nail into the board. This activity provides a wonderful Practical Life application. The foam block allows the practice of nailing into a surface which makes it easy to complete the activity successfully even for young children.

Extension 1

This extension is similar but utilizes golf tees in the hammering process. The tees work well for the activity and are somewhat larger and easier for children to handle. The tees can be combined with the mallet or the hammer.

Extension 2

Caution: Children should first master hammering using the floral foam block before moving to the block of wood.

This extension is very close to the first activity but increases the difficulty by adding a wooden board which is prepared with pre-drilled holes for the child to use in order to hammer the nails. With the addition of the hammer, the child can also practice using the back of the hammer head in order to remove the nails from the wood.

Extension 3

This extension takes the process of learning to hammer one step further by taking the activity outside. If you have a tree stump, this is a fun application. Simply take the nail and hammers and have the children hammer them into a tree stump. If a tree stump is not available you can have a large piece of wood cut so that there is a flat surface both on the top and the bottom. Set it securely on the ground to accommodate this activity. After hammering in the nails, have the child use the back of the hammer to remove them and prepare the activity to be repeated.

Matching Nuts and Bolts

Materials Needed

- ❖ Nuts and Bolts in Various Sizes
- ❖ Box (With Dividers if Available)

Presentation and Activity:

Take the nuts and bolts and match them together. Once a match is found, twist the nut onto the bolt and move it to a different section of the box. Look for another match and then repeat the activity. Once all of the nuts and bolts have been matched, twist all of the nuts back off of the bolts and set the pieces in separate compartments so that the activity may be repeated.

Locks and Latches Board

A locks and latches board can be expensive when purchased commercially; however, it can be easily constructed. Take a flat piece of scrap wood in a size that is easy for a child to hold and carry. Sand the board smooth. Then purchase some inexpensive locks, latches, and even a switch if desired, from a home improvement store or the hardware section of a discount store. Select locks and latches which require different skills to complete. Next, screw them to the board.

Materials Needed

❖ Locks and Latches Board

Presentation and Activity:

This activity can be demonstrated for the child in a Montessori style demonstration or it can be provided as an exploratory activity. As an exploratory activity, the child can work on it and "discover" how to open and close all of the locks and latches on the board.

Padlock Board

Materials Needed

❖ Various Sized Padlocks
❖ Keys to Locks
❖ Basket
❖ Display Tray

The locks can be mounted to a wood board such as the example. As an alternative, the locks and keys can simply be placed in a basket.

Presentation and Activity:

This activity can be demonstrated for the child in a Montessori style demonstration or it can be provided as an exploratory activity. As an exploratory activity, the child can work on it and "discover" how to insert the keys into the locks and which key opens which lock.

11
Nature and Outdoors

Nature Tray

Materials Needed

- ❖ Selected Natural Materials
- ❖ Display Tray

Presentation and Activity:

This activity works well as a shelf activity. It provides the opportunity for children to see, feel, and evaluate natural materials. It fits into the Practical Life, sensorial, and science materials within a Montessori environment. This activity is even more enjoyable if the children are allowed to go outdoors and select materials that they would like to include in the tray. It can also be utilized as an activity in which children bring materials they find in nature to share with other children in a classroom environment.

Nature Collage

Materials Needed

- ❖ Selected Natural Materials
- ❖ Styrofoam Plate
- ❖ Glue
- ❖ Work Tray

Presentation and Activity:

Take the children on a nature walk. While on the walk, have them select interesting things they would like to have in their collage such as rocks, sticks, leaves, grass, and flowers. When they return to the classroom they can create a collage of collected treasures. Take the Styrofoam plate, fill it with school glue, and then arrange the found items over the glue. Allow the glue to fully dry which can take a couple of days.

Arranging Flowers

Materials Needed

- ❖ Flowers (Fresh or Silk)
- ❖ Plastic Vase (or Multiple Vases if Desired)
- ❖ Display Tray

Presentation and Activity:

Take the cut flowers and arrange them inside the vase to make a beautiful arrangement. For fresh flowers, water can be added to the project. Enjoy the fun and beauty of arranging flowers.

This activity can be varied with different colors and types of flowers to celebrate different seasons. Silk flowers can be used without water for a shelf activity and available anytime. When arranging fresh flowers, this activity is best used as a center activity and replenished as needed.

Feeding Birds

Caution: Some children are allergic to peanuts; in this case choose another form of adhesive such as almond butter.

Materials Needed

- Pine Cone
- Peanut Butter (or Other Nut Butter)
- Wild Bird Seed
- Cord
- Spreader

Presentation and Activity:

Take the pine cone and cover it with peanut butter using the spreader or a blunt knife. Next, sprinkle the bird seeds over the pine cone. Tie the cord to the pine cone. Take the feeder outside and hang it from a tree branch using the cord. Enjoy watching the birds come and eat the food from this special bird feeder.

Notes: This is a very messy project. It is best completed on a table covered with newspaper or even completed outside.

Watering Plants

Materials Needed:

- Watering Can or a Water Hose
- Outdoor Plants, Lawn, or Garden

Presentation and Activity:

Let the child help with the care of the outdoor plants. Show the child how to water the plants gently so that it doesn't hurt to plants or disturb the soil. This is a simple concept and easy to complete. It creates important lessons and wonderful Practical Life applications with the simple act of caring for the outdoor plants.

Planting Seeds

Materials Needed

- ❖ Selected Seeds (Vegetable, Fruit, or Flower Seeds)
- ❖ Potting Soil
- ❖ Planter
- ❖ Water in a Small Pitcher
- ❖ Ladle, Shovel, or Large Spoon (to Scoop and Spread Soil)
- ❖ Work Tray

Presentation and Activity:

Fill the planter 2/3 of the way full using the ladle. Make a small indention in the potting soil with your fingers. Place the seed inside the indention. Cover up the seed and gently water the seed using the pouring skills to carefully control the water.

Place the planter in a window sill or outdoors. Enjoy the process of monitoring the growth, continuing to water, and enjoying the benefits and learning experience of growing a plant.

Extensions:

This can easily be extended to a complete outdoor activity where the seeds are planted directly into the ground. It is a wonderful project for children to create their own vegetable and fruit gardens. After these develop it can be extended into Practical Life lessons in harvesting, washing, and preparing food.

Egg cartons make a good planter for classrooms of children. Each individual space can be used as a planter for a child. Paper and plastic cups can also be used. These are not as authentic as a traditional planter but they are much more economical.

Commercial materials are available to create root view projects so that children can observe how plants are growing under the soil. An inexpensive application with all of the benefits would be to plant your seeds inside of empty CD cases and enjoy the observations that you can't see in a traditional planter. This application can also be adapted to using a paper towel rather than soil. The seeds will sprout inside the paper towel and it is easy to see what is happening without the dark colored soil.

More Simple Outdoor Practical Life Activities

- ❖ Teach your child how to care for pets (indoors or outdoors). Simple activities such as filling water and food bowls provide valuable lessons in caring for animals as well as building important fine motor skills. (When incorporating pets into a group environment, be aware of any children with allergies to pet dander.)

- ❖ Bird watching is a wonderful and educational activity. Simply watching the birds and observing behaviors is fun and educational. If you have binoculars, take those and make even closer observations. If your child really enjoys the bird activities, you may want to invest in a bird identification book so that he can learn to identify the different species of birds. This is also a good activity to combine with the Practical Life activity of making a bird feeder on page 106.

- ❖ Insects are fascinating to observe and can be found almost anywhere. Go for a walk. Take time to look and observe the surroundings. Watch ants as they make a trail or look carefully at a bug with a magnifying glass. Look around and observe nature then enhance those lessons with nonfiction books or online resources.

- ❖ Scooping up an insect for a closer observation can be a fascinating way to observe it up close. Take care, during your observation, not to harm the insect and then be sure to carefully release it back into its natural environment after observing it for a little while.

- ❖ Animal track identification is another fun and educational outdoor activity if you live in an area with wildlife or are close to a natural area or state park. Use books or online resources to help children identify the types of animals that left the tracks. Extend the animal tracks fun by using Plaster of Paris to create impressions of animal tracks that the children can keep.

- ❖ Plant Identification is another fun outdoor activity. Just as with animal track identification, children can learn to use resources and extend their knowledge of outdoor life. Plant samples can be taken back into the classroom or home and pressed for a fun project and a way to preserve the example for use in your nature materials.

- ❖ Use your imagination and include your children in your daily activities. It takes longer to complete activities with a child "helping" by your side but the benefits of time well spent together and the knowledge of a child absorbing the world around her is priceless.

Appendix: A
Grace and Courtesy

Manners and social graces are important elements of Montessori Practical Life. In Montessori programs, these skills are referred to as grace and courtesy. Rather than activities which are set on a shelf, these activities are explained and practiced daily. As they are practiced each day, they become a part of the Montessori and home environment and a beautiful part of a well mannered child. There are many elements of social graces the following list includes a number of those and a good place to start. Incorporate manners and appropriate social skills into your home, classroom, and life. Children learn what they see and will easily demonstrate that knowledge when raised with such skills.

- Appropriate Greetings
- Saying Please and Thank You
- Patiently Waiting
- Refraining from Interrupting Conversations
- How to Appropriately Gain Someone's Attention
- Cleaning Up After Themselves
- Helping with Chores
- How to Ask Permission
- How to Handle Disappointments with Dignity
- How to Answer and Talk on the Telephone
- Appropriate Words and Conversation
- Making Positive and Appropriate Comments
- Being Respectful to Others
- Appropriate Etiquette for Meals
- How to Cover a Sneeze
- How to Cover a Cough
- How to Blow a Nose
- Knocking on Doors Before Entering
- Respecting the Property of Others

Safety Lessons

It is also important to include safety lessons in all early childhood education programs. Some safety lessons to include are:

- Knowing Their Parent's Full Name and Phone Numbers
- Knowing Their Street Address, City, and State
- Safety with Regard to Strangers
- Not Going into Street Without a Trusted Grown Up
- Staying Away from Pools or Other Bodies of Water Unless with a Trusted Grown Up
- Staying Away from Trains and Train Tracks
- Fire Safety

Appendix B:

Material Sources for Building Your Practical Life Program

Materials for creating your own Practical Life activities can be obtained from many different sources. These are just some of the sources available for materials. The types of materials found at each source are included, as well as page numbers where appropriate, for specific examples of materials used in example photographs.

Wal-Mart: This is a good source for many Practical Life materials in areas such as the kitchen, linens, grocery, hardware, art, and other store departments.

Kitchen Section materials include items such as: condiment cups; small mixing bowls; ice trays; tongs; small ladles; juicers (p. 39); basters (p. 23); melon ball tools (p. 58); tiny skewers (p. 59); vegetable peelers (p. 62); a variety of graters; syrup pitchers (p. 32); creamer pitchers; salad cruet sets; egg slicers (p. 53); plastic dishes that look like glass (p. 22); wood cutting boards (p. 57); cookie cutters; silverware sorting trays; and laundry baskets (pp. 70, 71).

Linen and Home Section materials include: work mats (p. 11); baskets; various wire racks (pp. 69, 72); clothes pins (p. 72); dusting set materials; small sweeper sets (p. 3); lint rollers (p. 74); spray bottles (p. 74); dish towels; wash cloths; and lunch kits.

Grocery Section materials include: real food and food coloring. It is also a good source of dry products for scooping and pouring skills such as rice; beans; peas; cornmeal; and other grains.

Hardware Section materials include: nuts and bolts; locks and latches for boards; paint samples; hammers; and nails.

Art Supply Section materials include: icing spreaders (p. 57); felt and buttons for creating the buttoning materials (p. 82); paint pallet (p. 23); chenille sticks (p. 82); beads; decorative scrapbook paper; envelopes; glue; pencils; pencil sharpeners; cording; buttons; floral foam blocks; and silk flowers.

Other Sections include various other materials such as: personal care items including combs; brushes; toothbrushes; and mirrors. The toy section can provide materials such as the baby and bathtub set (p. 84), and the sporting goods section can provide materials such as golf tees.

Montessori Services & For Small Hands: These are available both by catalog and online. This is a wonderful source for Montessori Practical Life materials in miniature size shown in the example photos. These materials include: tiny baskets; wood plates and bowls (p. 15); tiny wood spoons (pp. 17, 22); mustard spoons (p. 15); ladles (p. 19); small stainless steel scoops (p. 18); tiny sifters and strainers (pp. 20, 42); little tongs (p. 22); turners (p. 26); child size pitchers and cups; wavy choppers (p. 57); tiny vegetable scrubbers (p. 62); sandwich cutters (p. 65); and child size wood mallets (p. 102).

Dollar Tree: This is a good source for many Practical Life materials that are inexpensive. Dollar Tree online is also a very good source for schools and child care centers who need larger quantities of items to fill their shelves. Online purchases have a large variety of items that require purchasing specified quantities. This is a good source for baskets; display trays; plastic serving dishes (p. 25); plastic trays and flower vases that look like glass (pp. 33, 109); cups; dishes; flatware; flatware sorting trays; ice trays; linens; placemats; kitchen towels; personal care items such as combs, brushes, toothbrushes, and mirrors; various dusting materials; small sweeper sets (p. 73); lint rollers; miscellaneous art supplies; packages of rocks and marbles; and silk flowers.

Restaurant Supply Stores: This is a good source for fun and creative kitchen Practical Life materials. These stores often have beautiful and interesting dishware to make beautiful sets. It is a good place to find items that look like glass and pottery but are not breakable. These stores also carry many things in small sizes which are perfect for Practical Life skills and small hands. Examples of materials found at restaurant supply stores include: plastic food trays for display and work areas; condiment cups; small plates; plastic pieces that look like beautiful pottery and glass; small plastic pitchers and 5 oz cups (p. 31); tea pots (p. 30); small cream pitchers; tiny espresso cups (p. 40); and syrup pitchers.

These stores often have unique items and Asian inspired patterns such as small platter and tiny dipping bowls (pp. 19, 47); tiny rice bowls (p. 22); tiny sake sets (p. 32); miniature sets of bowls; soup spoons and unique surprises such as the boat set in our scooping activity (p 23). Each store will have a different variety of items. It is a fun place to find treasures that make your Practical Life shelves even more unique and engaging for children.

Your own Home and Garage: This is a good source for many items at no additional cost. These items include: dishes; flatware; placemats; wash cloths; kitchen towels; pots; cups; bowls; dusting materials; clothes to create dressing activities; and baskets.

Grocery Store: This is a good source for projects using real food as well as dry products for scooping and pouring skills. These items include rice; beans; peas; cornmeal; and other grains.

Nature: This is a wonderful source for natural authentic materials you can have for free including: sand; sea shells; rocks; sticks; pine cones; and acorns (p. 108).

Party Stores: This is a good source for authentic looking materials that look like glass or stoneware but are not breakable. Exact materials available will vary by the specific store.

Pier 1: This is a good source for creative and beautiful kitchenware for Practical Life activities. Examples of materials available from this store include: appetizer serving dishes (p. 26); unique bowls such as the fish bowls on page 25; cheese slicers (p. 46); small spoons; and placemats.

Tractor Supply Company: This is a good source for old fashioned looking buckets both large and small such as the metal buckets in example photos for washing dishes (p. 69); clipping clothes pins (p. 72); and holding potting soil (p. 112).

Building Supply Store: This is a good source for locks and latches to create activity boards (p. 105); paint sample cards; carpet samples; nuts and bolts; wood; hammers; nails; and wood blocks.

World Market: This is a good source for unique bowls; display items; small silverware; tiny dishes (p. 24); cheese slicers; small spoons; and tiny skewers (p. 59).

Discount School Supply: This is a good source for numerous materials which can be utilized in Montessori Practical Life skills as well as traditional preschool materials. Examples of materials from this resource include: plastic trays; chenille sticks; collections of sea shells; beads; child scissors; glue; and other art materials.

Children's Magazines such as National Geographic Kids & My Big Backyard: These are good sources for reading and then after you are finished reading them they make wonderful materials to use in cutting; pasting; and creating with realistic and authentic pictures.

Garage Sales & Resale Stores: This is a good source for inexpensive household items for all areas of Practical Life materials.

Think like a preschool teacher and save items such as leftover wood boxes from toy and activity sets or other packaging: These are great for sorting and working with material. Many children's activities come in nice packaging including some in wooden boxes such as the box on page 101 used for sorting nuts and bolts. These can be saved and used as display trays for your shelf materials. Also, save baskets left over from gift baskets or packaging materials. These make perfect baskets to set on your shelves and contain your Montessori Practical Life materials. The variety of pretty baskets enhances the beauty of the shelf materials.

Andrea Hendon Busch, Ed.D. is an educational specialist with a doctorate degree in Educational Administration and Supervision. She is a certified public school teacher, certified public school administrator, and a state licensed child care director. Dr. Busch has been an educator for 21 years. She is an experienced classroom teacher, early childhood administrator, and curriculum designer. She holds a Montessori Preschool and Kindergarten Teaching Credential. Dr. Busch designed, founded, managed, and directed a successful Montessori-Based child care center where she implemented the Practical Life skills included in this book.

Dr. Busch has studied extensively in the field of early childhood education. She has researched programs and philosophies in the United States as well as international programs including travel to China to visit preschools and consulting with educators in China.

Dr. Busch provides lectures, training, and consulting services for parents, seminars, and child care centers. She can be contacted at andreab@windsonghollowranch.com for additional information on speaking, training, and consulting programs.

Other books by Andrea Hendon Busch, Ed.D. are available at Amazon.com.

The Secrets of Managing a Successful Childcare Center

Process Art: Paint

Made in the USA
Middletown, DE
20 January 2018